THE YACHTSMAN'S EMERGENCY HANDBOOK

THE YACHTSMAN'S EMERGENCY HANDBOOK

The Complete Survival Manual

Neil Hollander & Harald Mertes

Angus & Robertson · Publishers

Angus & Robertson • Publishers
London • Sydney • Melbourne • Singapore • Manila

First published in Great Britain by Angus & Robertson (UK) Ltd,
10 Earlham Street, London, in 1980

ISBN 0 207 95815 7

Printed in USA

Phototypeset in VIP Helvetica by
Trident Graphics Limited, Reigate, Surrey
Composition by Sarisberie Designs
20 Oatmeal Row, Salisbury, Wiltshire

To Gilbert and Heinz
who advised us:

*"When in danger or in doubt,
Sail in circles, scream and shout!"*

Foreword

by Edward Heath

Most books about boats, whether sail or motor, whether racing or cruising, tell us how to go about handling them the right way. We enjoy reading them during the winter months and a few, a very select few, we take with us on board when the season begins.

But however much we read and study, however hard we try, things don't always go well. Everyone who puts to sea ought to know the capabilities of the boat and the crew; ought to keep within their limitations as far as tide and weather are concerned; ought above all to respect the sea and to recognize the infinite variety of moods of which it is capable. Nevertheless, at times we are taken unawares to a greater or lesser degree.

The Yachtsman's Emergency Handbook is designed to help us cope with just such a situation. In this it is unusual. It tells us what to do when things go wrong. It does so with clarity, succinctness and brevity, illustrated with practical diagrams easily understood at a glance.

This is a handbook which all owners and crews will want to possess. To get full value from its pages will demand intensive study, thought and discussion during the off season so that the information it contains will become absorbed, memorized and ready for instant use in an emergency. It is a book which it is essential to have on board in case of need, no matter how small the navigator's bookshelf.

May you never have to make use of its advice. But if you do, may it help you to overcome difficulties, pass through danger and moor safely in harbour.

Introduction

The idea for this book arrived during a storm – a Force 9 gale in the Gulf of Lyons. Like many storms one encounters at sea, foam and fury suddenly seemed to come from nowhere. Rumbling black clouds raced across the sky and what had been a tranquil four-day passage from Sète to Ibiza was quickly twisted into a *Mistral* struggle. Swimming suits off – oilskins on, genoa down – trisail up, fishing lines in – sea anchor out.

As the seas rose higher and higher, our over-aged cutter began to shudder and creak. Her timbers started to work and, to our horror, caulking fell out like dandruff.

A plank separated from the stem. Then another.

The backstay parted.

All three bilge pumps packed up.

So did the engine, roller reefing and the galley stove.

A hurried search through a shelf of soggy yachting books yielded no quick solutions – in fact, no solutions at all. The emphasis was clearly on the 'buy' and 'buy not' and the 'do' and 'do not'. For some reason, the vital 'when' and 'if' were hard to find. With chaos whirling about us, there wasn't time to skim through densely printed pages of anecdote and theory, searching for bits of emergency advice.

Unfortunately, we were on our own, and that was by no means comforting. Angry seas inspire little confidence. To make matters worse, at that moment in our sailing lives there was too much we didn't know and hadn't tried. Yet, somehow – certainly more by luck than by experience – our guesses outweighed our mistakes, and our instincts kept us afloat and alive. Jury-rigged, jury-sailed and jury-fed we listed into Ibiza a week later.

Not everything was repaired at sea, of course. Far from it. However, we did manage to keep the boat in what might be generously called a 'a serviceable order'. It was only later we realized that that was exactly what we should have done.

Since then, wherever we have sailed – the Atlantic, Caribbean and Pacific – we have made a habit of noting down bits and pieces of emergency experience; our own, and also those of other yachtsmen which were passed to us over mooring lines and bars: tips, short-cuts, the makeshift and make-do, the impractical essential and the essential impractical.

The result – this book – is by no means complete, nor is it a panacea, but we do hope it will point someone in trouble in the right direction – if not with a solution, then at least with a few hints as to where he might look for one.

We have tried to keep the text as pragmatic and terse as possible, maintaining the perspective that whatever the emergency – dismasting, engine failure, grounding or a man overboard – it is occurring at the moment. The immediate, crucial question is: What must be done? Now! First!

We have left out such actions as 'Call all hands on deck!' 'Put on Lifejackets!' or 'Tend to the Injured!' as they are – we should hope – too obvious to mention. Our concern has been with the less obvious – the difficult decision and the logical – or in some cases apparently illogical – actions that follow.

For these, we have drawn freely from the large storehouse of accumulated knowledge, that which lives in the minds and hearts of yachtsmen and sailors and also that which is filed on dusty library shelves.

Hence, we have many people to thank.

Certainly, without them this book would never be.

Acknowledgements

Tom Streithorst (Alkatraz), Charles Malcolm (Ancela), J. H. Plettenberg (Andromeda), Chantal Izard (Audonien), Nigel Dalton (Blackbeard), Liljana de Pauli (Chica), Jesse and Stephen (Double Eagle), Brian McGarry and Joe Menell (Fiona), Bob Taylor (Freedom), Tony Badger (Gaucho), Herbert Gossmann (Jonas), Helmut and Anne Möhrmann (Kleiner Bär), Simone Darmon (La Marie Garlande), Heinz Tenbrinck (La Paloma), James Irvitie (Mathew), Rolando Soto (Media Luna), Paul and Martha Setram (Mercedes), Howard Benett (Nana), Alain Relmy (Nayla), Kurt M. Englebert (Peer Gynt), Herman Biasotti (Sol), Ferdl and Susi Kassler (Venceremos).

Our medical advisors were Nurse Mary Jo Nelson, Dr. Henry Campion of the American Hospital of Paris, and Dr. Günther Dötsch, Dr. Max Krämer and Dr. Adolf Keuser of Koblenz.

Many people aided us in ways too numerous to mention: Sabine Bäcker, Irmela Brender, Don Manuel Campos, Nadia Christensen, Otmar Dills, the de Pauli family, Maggie Hemingway, Dennis Ing, Lilly Libedinsky, Stephen Paul, Malcolm Robson, Charles Roth, Joachim and Brigitte Scheid, Norman Stokle, the Tepa family of Bora Bora, and Liz, Penny Esperth and Sally of the Cruising Association.

Brookes & Gatehouse, Citizens of the Sea, Cruising Association, Electronic Laboratories, Günter Schleich, Ocean Cruising Club, RFD Inflatables, Rhein-Mosel Yacht Club, Switlik Parachute Company, Ernest Benn for permission to re-print the Salvage agreement from **Law For Small Boats.**

A

Abandon ship!

See also: Evacuation

Alongside a larger vessel ■ 1

If a choice exists, allow yourself to be hoisted on board, rather than climb a ladder against the ship's side.

Leave the boat from well forward or well aft of the mast so as not to be struck or tangled by the spars or rigging.

Time your moment of departure so that you leave on the crest of a wave, letting the boat fall away from you.

WARNING:

Going alongside a freighter or tanker risks being dismasted.

Into a liferaft

See: Liferaft

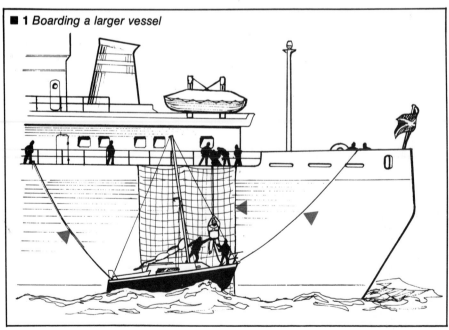

■ 1 *Boarding a larger vessel*

Jumping in the water

Loosen clothing.

If wearing a lifejacket, hold it down and away from your chin.

Leave from the windward side, since more than likely the boat will drift faster than you can swim.

Jump feet first, legs together, with your mouth closed. If jumping from a height, hold nose and cover mouth.

Swim clear of the boat.

If there is oil in the water

Swim underwater if possible. Keep your eyes tightly shut. When coming up for air, protect your eyes, nose and mouth with your hands as you break the surface. Use your arms to sweep away the oil, turn your back to the wind, hold your breath and dive again.

When swimming on the surface, use a rapid breast stroke to thrust the oil away from your face.

In cold water

Enter the water fully clothed.

Empty your pockets of all weights.

Do not remove boots, shoes or mittens.

If possible, tape or tightly tie wrists, waist and ankles so that water trapped inside will have a wet-suit effect. For perhaps the first quarter of an hour, clothes will provide some buoyancy and later when soaked become excellent insulation. Contrary to expectation, wet clothes in the water weigh no more than dry clothes ashore.

Float. Do *not* swim. Exercise will only increase your heat loss, thus depriving you of energy.

NOTE:

Immediately after entering the water it will probably be difficult to breathe normally. However, this will pass within a few minutes.

Rescue by helicopter

METHOD 1

Keep the boat on a predictable course.

Make your exit from the stern.

If possible, release the standing backstay, running backstays, and other lines that might foul the transfer.

Show a green light or flag when you are ready to leave; a red light or flag if you are not.

Do *not* make fast the line or wire lowered from the helicopter.

Normally the helicopter will lower a harness. If not, prepare a bosun's chair.

For an emergency bosun's chair. **See: Climbing the mast.**

METHOD 2

Make contact with the helicopter from a dinghy or liferaft towed astern.

Accidents

See also: Salvage towing

If an accident occurs

By law and custom the vessels are bound to stand-by and render aid to each other and exchange the following:

Names.

Home ports.

Ports from which they have come.

Ports to which they are going.

Legal action

This can nearly always be started in the country whose flag flies on the stern of the ship being prosecuted.

British courts allow collision actions to be brought if the guilty ship, irrespective of its nationality, is in a British port at the time the action is brought.

French and German courts claim jurisdiction if the damaged yacht flies their flag, even though the guilty vessel may be foreign. In principle, a ship is a part of the country, and a collision with a French or German vessel is said to have occurred in either France or Germany.

NOTE:

A violation of 'The Rules of the Road' **(See: Collision)** is no longer a presumption of guilt. Courts now examine all circumstances to determine the responsibility for the accident.

Aground

On a weather shore – Back the jib

With the wind abaft the beam – Gybe

On a lee shore – Drop or luff all sails at once

Usually, *the easiest way off* is the same route one went on.

Start the engine

Apply moderate power. Your own wake, rolling under the stern may lift the boat free.

WARNING:

If the tide is ebbing

There may be little time before the boat is hopelessly aground. For example, with a tidal range of 3–4m., a fall of 10cm. in 10 minutes is not unusual. With a falling tide, unless one gets off almost immediately, it is better to prepare the boat to dry out than to waste valuable time trying to break free. **See: Drying out.**

If the tide is rising

The danger lies in being swept further aground. Free the sheets, and take down all sail. Anchors should be set at once, and, depending on sea and weather conditions, both fore and aft. **See: Anchoring.**

NOTE:

High water at night is usually slightly higher than high water during the day.

Heeling

Heeling to one side may reduce the draft and free the boat. Should the keel be stuck in mud this may also break the suction hold.

WARNING:

Boats with bilge keels should not be heeled ■ 3. Once the boat is heeled, her draft increases.

NOTE:

The moment a heeled boat breaks free, the sails, the engine, or a bow anchor should be ready for a seaward course.

METHOD 1 Heeling with weights

Use the weight of the crew on the crosstrees, end of the boom, or hanging over the side.

Tie a weight, such as an anchor, dinghy filled with water, or water cans to the end of the boom and run it out abeam. Support the boom with the main halyard attached to the boom end ■ 4.

■ 2 *Heeling decreases the draft*

■ 3 *Heeling increases the draft*

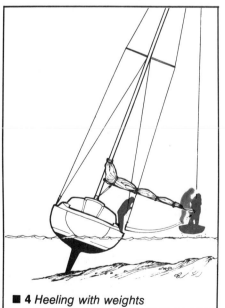

■ 4 *Heeling with weights*

METHOD 2 Heeling with an anchor

Lay the anchor chain on the deck to list the boat.

Lay out the kedge anchor and attach its warp to the main, jib, or spinnaker halyard. Take the fall of the halyard to a winch **■ 5**.

WARNING:

Masthead fittings are not designed for lateral pull. To reduce strain, a strong line can be attached to the end of the halyard and the free end rove through a snatch block on the kedge warp, then taken to a cockpit winch **■ 5**. This will also increase the holding power of the anchor.

METHOD 3 Heeling with backed sails

Back the jib and/or mainsail thereby heeling the boat to leeward **■ 6**.

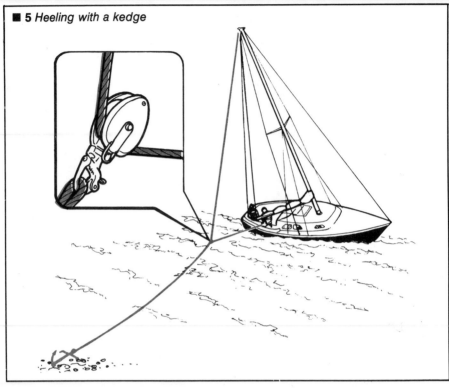

■ **5** *Heeling with a kedge*

■ **6** *Heeling with backed sails*

NOTE:

Without an anchor set, this method tends to push the boat further ashore.

METHOD 4 Heeling with the aid of a towboat

Tie the towrope loosely around the mast, then hoist the bight to the hounds with the main halyard ■ **7, 8**.

In this case do *not* pass the end of a halyard to the towboat as the strain generated by a large motor boat could easily endanger the mast.

NOTE:

For short fin keels

Rocking the boat back and forth and pivoting, in addition to heeling, can often slew the boat free.

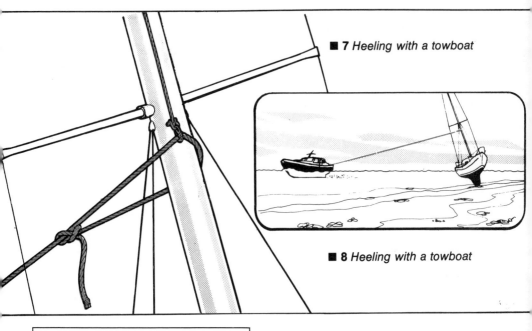

■ **7** *Heeling with a towboat*

■ **8** *Heeling with a towboat*

Lightening the boat

Empty water tanks.

Internal ballast, spare anchors and chain can be heaved over the side buoyed, and retrieved later.

All unnecessary crew members can be put in the dinghy.

NOTE:

Boats with long keels usually have their deepest draft aft. Consequently, moving crew and weight to the bow may be enough to shift the balance. This, combined with poling, using the engine, or pulling on a seaward anchor may be enought to free the boat.

■ **9** *Redistributing the boat's weight*

Kedging off

Set the kedge anchor from the dinghy.
See: Anchoring – A dragging anchor

Take the kedge warp to the anchor winch,
cockpit winch, or a block and tackle. **See:
Block and tackle**

Hauling off

Use the kedge anchor to heel the boat

*Use the bow anchor to haul the boat
free*

Lay out the kedge anchor and tie the warp
to the main halyard. Do not exert too

much force on the halyard as it may
damage the mast.

Lay out the bow anchor, and tie the chain
or warp to a winch or block and tackle.

Heel and pivot the boat at the same time
■ **10.**

NOTE:

If two warps need to be connected, use a
Carrick bend. **See: Knots**

WARNING:

If aground on hard rock, do not try to haul
free as this could easily damage the boat.
Instead prepare to dry out. **See: Drying
out**

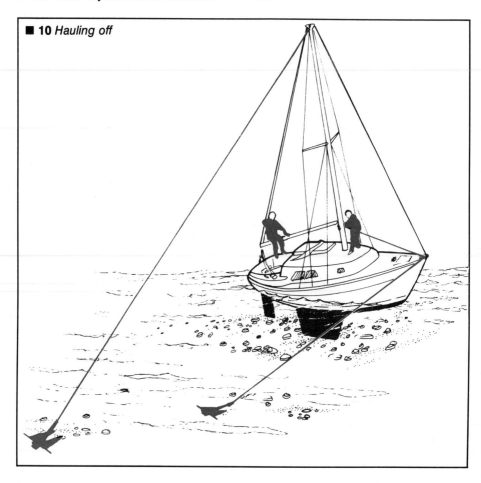

■ **10** *Hauling off*

Wakes and waves

The passing of another ship, especially a big one, can produce a wave large enough to free the boat momentarily.

A speed boat moving back and forth, even at low speeds, can have the same effect.

WARNING:

The boat may lift on a wake or wave and then crash down violently, possibly damaging herself or throwing the crew off balance.

Pushing and lifting

Besides lightening the boat, the muscle-power of a few crew members in the water often equals a strong winch. The person in the water should be fully clothed, wearing boots or shoes and gloves. His most powerful stance is under the bows, pushing backwards and upwards with his back. With bilge keels and light displacement craft, the best place is under the quarter.

If there is no possibility of re-floating the boat

See: Drying out

If the boat is in danger of breaking up

See: Scuttling

A–hull

See: Heavy weather

Aluminium repair

Leaks and holes

Repairing a small crack or tear

These can be filled with mastic, filler, cold solder, glass fibre or epoxy resin.

Repairing a larger rent

These will have to be patched.

Drill a small hole at each end of the crack to prevent it from continuing.

Cut the aluminium patch in a round or oval shape with at least 5cm. of overlap. If necessary, for short periods of time, any metal can be used.

Slightly bevel the outside edges of the patch.

Drill holes around the edges no more than 5cm. apart.

Shape the patch to the form of the hull with a rubber mallet.

Placing the patch on the outside of the hull is usually easier, but inside patching will permit the crack to be filled and sanded later to maintain a smooth hull form.

Clean and lightly sand the area around the hole or crack.

Using the patch as a template, mark the holes in the hull, then drill them.

Cover the inside of the patch with mastic or bedding compound.

Rivet the patch to the hull either with a rivet gun or a hammer and metal block.

NOTE:

If no mastic or bedding compound is available a watertight gasket can also be made from sailcloth, a towel, or a rag well greased or soaked in paint, primer, or bitumen.

Dents ■ 11

Small dents

These can be pounded out using a rubber mallet and a hard wood or metal block. Pounding should begin on the edge of the dent and move in concentric circles.

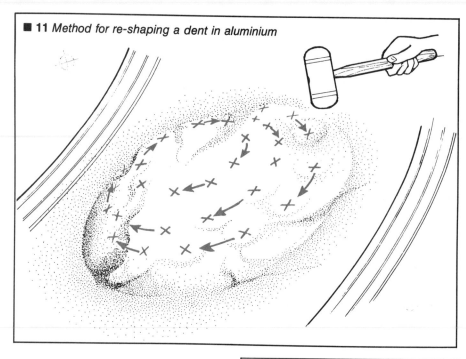

■ 11 *Method for re-shaping a dent in aluminium*

Larger dents

Those which may have stretched the metal, often need a hole drilled in the centre before they can be pounded back into shape. In this case, a patch must be riveted into place afterwards.

Alongside
See: Berthing

Anchoring

Anchoring signals

A vessel at anchor by day

A large black ball is hoisted into the rigging in the fore part of the vessel **■ 12**.

A vessel at anchor by night

Small boats – one white, all-round light visible two miles.

■ 12 *Daytime anchor signals*

■ 13 *Boats more than 50 metres in length*

Boats more than 50 metres in length –
must also show an after light lower than
the forward one ■ 13.

Boats more than 100 metres in length –
must also exhibit their deck lights ■ 14.

Oilrigs

An all-round white light visible for ten
miles and a red light at each corner visible
for two miles ■ 15.

All lights flash 'U' every 15 seconds.

■ 14 *Boats more than 100 metres*

■ 15 *Oilrigs*

International Code of Signals

'Y'

YANKEE

'I AM DRAGGING MY ANCHOR!' ■ 16.

For anchoring signals in fog or conditions
of restricted visibility. **See: Fog**

Yellow

Red

Yellow

Red

■ 16

Anchoring principles

Type of bottom

Sand: CQR or Danforth

Gravel: CQR or Danforth
Mud: CQR
A hard bottom: Fisherman
Rocks: Fisherman

To identify the character of the bottom, consult a nautical chart or **See: Echo sounders**

Scope

The ratio of water depth to anchor cable length should be:

Rope – Under favourable conditions 6:1
           Under unfavourable conditions 8:1
Chain – Under favourable conditions 4:1
           Under unfavourable conditions 5:1

Chain should make up at least $\frac{1}{4}$ of the anchor cable. This greatly increases holding power, acts as a shock absorber and prevents chafe on the bottom.

Windage

The wind's pressure on the boat rises along a steep curve as the Beaufort scale increases. An anchor set, for example, when the wind is Force 4 will have nearly *twice* the pressure on it at Force 5. Between Force 6 and 7 the pressure will nearly *double* again, and between Force 7 and 9 *double* once more.

A windage alarm ■ 17

A length of cord or line is tied to the chain, and the other end to a deck fitting so that the line bears the strain on the chain.

Several metres of chain are laid out on the deck.

When the wind increases, the line breaks and the loose chain runs out with a rattle and snap.

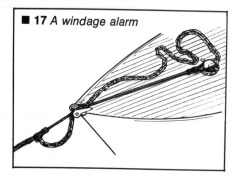

■ **17** *A windage alarm*

In a veering wind

Drop a second bow anchor underfoot in the direction towards which the wind is expected to veer ■ **18A**.

As the wind veers, and the boat swings, pay out the second anchor warp ■ **18B**, until the boat rides back safely on both anchors ■ **18C**.

NOTE:

In a crowded anchorage, anchor near boats using similar ground tackle i.e. chain near chain, warp near warp. They will swing in the same manner as you do.

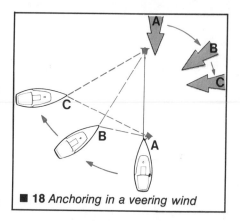

■ **18** *Anchoring in a veering wind*

Anchoring in strong tides or changing currents

METHOD 1 Anchors fore and aft

First drop the bow anchor upstream ■ **19A**.

Drift back to about double the length of the needed anchor cable, and dig in the anchor.

Drop the stern anchor ■ **19B**.

Pay out cable astern while winching or motoring upstream into position ■ **19C**.

For the length of the chain or warp required. **See: A dragging anchor**

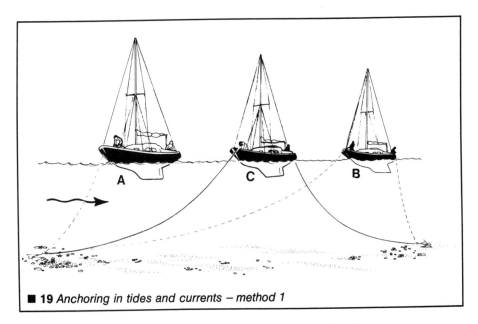

■ **19** *Anchoring in tides and currents – method 1*

WARNING:

If there is a lee-going ebb or flood the strongest anchor should be set in the direction which will bear the most strain.

METHOD 2 Two bow anchors

First drop the bow anchor upstream ■ **20A**.

Drift back to about double the length of the needed anchor line.

Drop the second anchor ■ **20B**.

Winch or motor upstream, taking in the first anchor cable until in position.

Shackle the second anchor line on to the first anchor chain ■ **20C**.

Lay out an additional 4–6 metres of chain, so that the keel will not foul the second anchor cable.

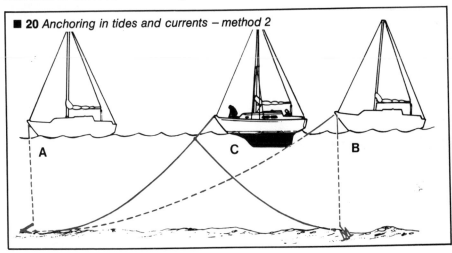

■ **20** *Anchoring in tides and currents – method 2*

Anchoring in heavy weather or on a lee shore

METHOD 1 Backing the anchor ■ 21

Attach the kedge to a length of chain and shackle it to the main anchor ring.

Drop the kedge first, then while going astern release the main anchor.

NOTE:

The length of the kedge chain should be slightly longer than the water depth, so that when retrieving the anchors one can be hoisted on board after the other.

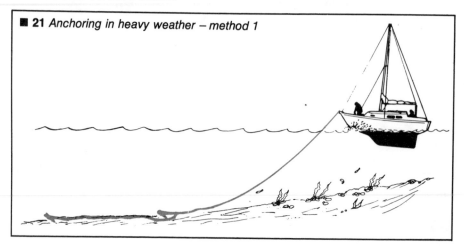

■ 21 *Anchoring in heavy weather – method 1*

METHOD 2 Double anchoring ■ 22

Shackle a second anchor on to the chain of the strongest anchor.

The distance between anchors should be roughly 10 metres, more for longer scope.

Do *not* drop both anchors at the same time.

This method should increase the holding power of the first anchor by about 100%.

Additional holding power can be added by sliding a weight down the chain. **See: A dragging anchor**

WARNING:

1 – The Samson post may need to be reinforced with a lashing to the mast.

2 – The chain's bitter end should be

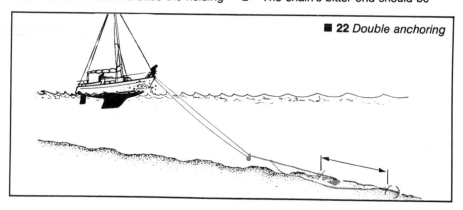

■ 22 *Double anchoring*

secured in the chain locker with a lashing, in case the wind shifts and it is necessary to cut and run.

If the boat is yawing or lying at a difficult angle to the seas, this can be eased by

Leaving the main or mizzen hoisted and sheeted amidships.

Hanking a jib on to the backstay and sheeting it amidships.

Attaching a spring from the quarter to the anchor cable.

Steering the boat as if she were underway.

A dragging anchor

To determine if the anchor is dragging lower a lead-line over the side until the weight touches bottom. Attach the end to a deck fitting and wait to see which way the line 'grows' ■ **23, 24**.

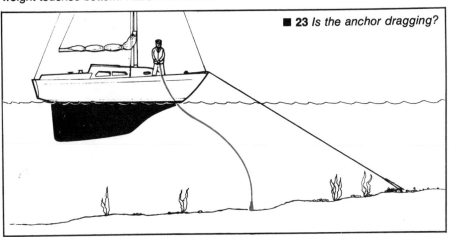

■ **23** *Is the anchor dragging?*

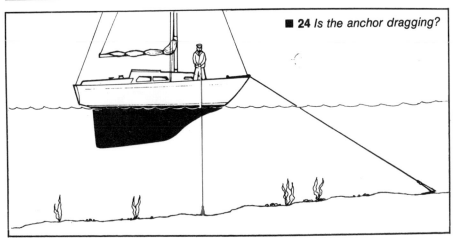

■ **24** *Is the anchor dragging?*

The lead-line can also be rigged as a 'frying pan' alarm ■ 25.

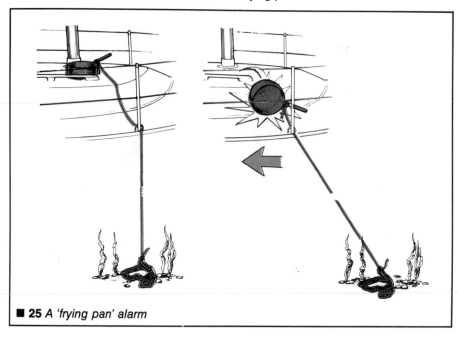

■ 25 *A 'frying pan' alarm*

If the anchor is dragging

Pay out more chain and/or rope.

Attach a weight – a piece of internal ballast, bucket of loose chain, or a string of shackles and rigging screws of at least 10 kilogrammes – to the anchor warp with a large shackle. Then allow the weight to ride down the warp ■ 26, 27, 28.

The object is to make the pull on the anchor as nearly horizontal as possible.

The weight should be far enough along the line so that the bow will not be heavy.

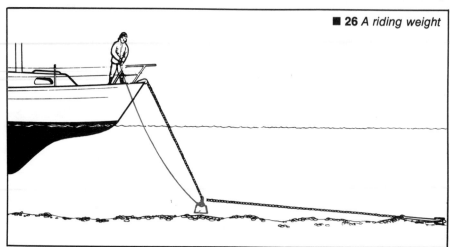

■ 26 *A riding weight*

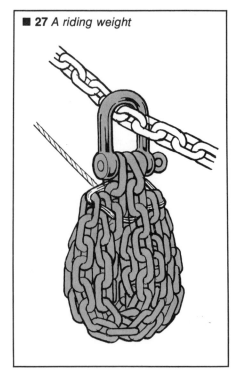

■ 27 *A riding weight*

■ 28 *A riding weight*

If the anchor continues to drag

Set a second anchor.

The angle between the two anchor lines should be about 30 degrees. This will provide *double* the holding power of a single anchor. However, as the angle increases, holding power decreases, until at an angle of 120 degrees between the anchor lines the holding power is the same as that of a single anchor laid out to windward.

Setting a second anchor under sail

Back the jib **■ 29A**.

Steer the boat as far as possible to one side **■ 29B**.

Drop the second anchor, then lie back on it.

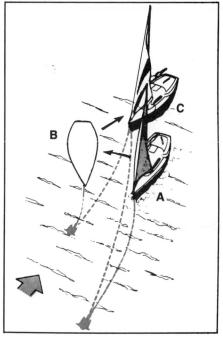

■ 29 *Setting a second anchor under sail*

Setting a second anchor by dinghy

Lash the anchor securely over the dinghy's transom ■ **30**.

Place the warp in the dinghy and pay it out gradually. The warp should be long enough to allow for the dinghy's drift. If necessary, a smaller line can be attached to the anchor warp, on the boat, then hauled in after the anchor is dropped.

Never row out chain. Instead, anchor the dinghy, and haul the chain to it on the warp. Then attach the chain to the anchor.

■ **30** *Setting an anchor by dinghy*

A fouled anchor

METHOD 1

Bring the bow directly over the anchor so that the chain is tight and vertical.

Secure the chain.

Rock the boat, fore to aft, in order to use the boat's buoyancy to break the anchor out.

METHOD 2

Sail or motor over the anchor and attempt to pull it out from the other direction.

METHOD 3

Pass a ring, a large loop, or better still, a bit of chain over the anchor chain and, using a dinghy, tow it down until it reaches the anchor's crown. Then attempt to raise the anchor from the dinghy ■ **31**.

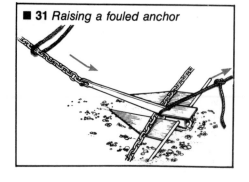

■ **31** *Raising a fouled anchor*

METHOD 4

Using a line or chain approximately three times the length of the anchor chain, tow the loop as far down the chain as possible. Drop the dinghy's anchor and when it is firmly dug-in, then attempt to break the boat's anchor free ■ **32**.

METHOD 5

If the anchor is fouled on another boat's chain

Attempt to raise *both* the anchor and the chain as high as possible.

Pass a line around the chain and secure it to the boat.

Free the anchor by hand or by dropping it.

Then release the chain ■ **33**.

METHOD 6

If the chain and anchor cannot be raised

A kedge or dinghy anchor will serve as a grapple.

Once the anchor is hooked, the line can be either pulled from different directions or taken back to the boat where the chain and anchor can be raised with a winch ■ **34**.

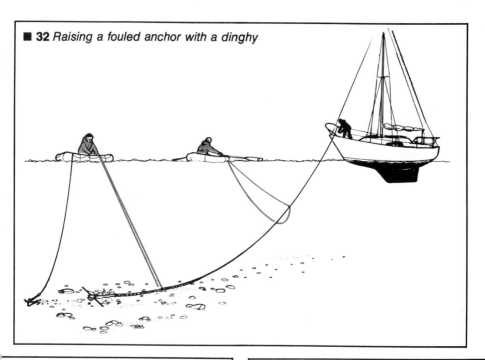

■ 32 *Raising a fouled anchor with a dinghy*

■ 33 *Raising a fouled anchor from on board*

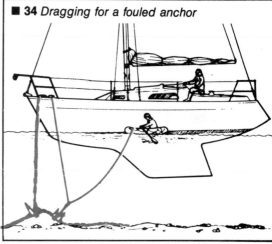

■ 34 *Dragging for a fouled anchor*

A tripping line ■ 35

Many anchoring problems, particularly in new or unknown anchorages, can be prevented by attaching a *tripping line* to the anchor's crown. This line can be either buoyed or led back to the boat and secured to the anchor chain.

When buoyed, a short length of light chain

will hold the line straight in the water, making it less likely to be cut by a passing craft.

■ **35** *A tripping line*

Single-handed anchoring

Anchor release ■ 36

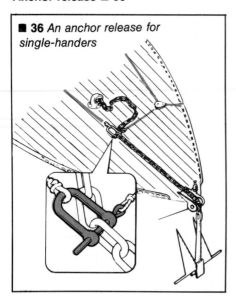

■ **36** *An anchor release for single-handers*

A large shackle is tied with a strop to a deck fitting.

The anchor chain passes through the shackle and is held in place by a large well-greased split pin or piece of rod. Cord or line is attached to the head of the pin and run through blocks back to the cockpit.

Procedure

The anchor is slung over the bow, held in place by the shackle release.

Pulling the cord removes the pin and the anchor chain runs free.

A makeshift anchor ■ 37

Materials

Two sharpened pieces of hard wood.

A weight, such as a stone or piece of internal ballast.

Line or wire cable.

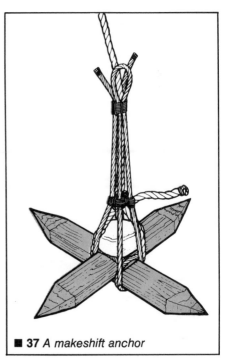

■ **37** *A makeshift anchor*

A makeshift CQR ■ 38

Materials

A fisherman's anchor.

Line or wire.

A metal bucket.

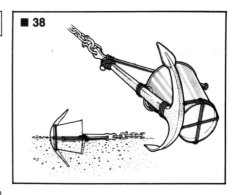

■ 38

Antibiotics

After entering the body, antibiotics go to the area of infection and either kill the harmful bacteria or retard their growth so that the normal protection system of the body can function properly.

WARNING:

When taking antibiotics, do *not* drink alcohol.

For chest, throat, and ear infections, boils, infected cuts,* and venereal disease†

	Dosage
England Tetracycline	500mg. 4 times/ day *for* 8 days

	Dosage
France Tetracycline	500mg. 4 times/ day *for* 8 days

	Dosage
Germany Doxycyclin	100mg. 2 times/ day *for* 8 days

If no improvement after 3–4 days, change to:

	Dosage
England Ampicillin	500mg. 4 times/ day *for* 8 days

	Dosage
France Totapen	500mg. 4 times/ day *for* 8 days

	Dosage
Germany Binotal	500mg. 4 times/ day *for* 8 days

WARNING:

If allergic to penicillin, do *not* take Ampicillin. Take Erythromycin instead with the same dosage.

*NOTE:

For infected cuts, take *only* Tetracyline.

†NOTE:

For venereal disease, begin with 1.5 grams of Tetracycline, then continue at 500mg. four times a day, for the next four days.

NOTE:

Oral antibiotics often irritate the gastrointestinal tract, and may cause nausea, vomiting and diarrhoea.

For urinary tract infections

	Dosage
England	
Septrin	2 tablets 2 times/ day

	Dosage
France	
Bactrim	2 tablets 2 times/ day

	Dosage
Germany	
Bactrim	2 tablets 2 times/ day

For dysentery

	Dosage
England	
Tetracycline	500mg. 4 times/ day for 10 days

	Dosage
France	
Tetracycline	500mg. 4 times/ day for 10 days

	Dosage
Germany	
Doxycyclin	100mg. 2 times/ day for 10 days

If no improvement after 3–4 days, take:

	Dosage
England	
Flagyl	800mg. 3 times/ day for 10 days

	Dosage
France	
Flagyl	800mg. 3 times/ day for 10 days

	Dosage
Germany	
Flagyl	800mg. 3 times/ day for 10 days

For skin infection and minor infected wounds

Before applying topical antibiotics wash the area with warm, soapy water and antiseptic. **See: Antiseptics**

Topical antibiotics

	Dosage
England	
Neomycin	5mg. Apply 2–4 times/day
Bacitracin zinc	500 units/ gram Apply 2–4 times/day

Dosage	
France	
Neomycin	5mg. Apply 2–4 times/day
Bacitracin zinc	
	500 units/ gram Apply 2–4 times/day

Dosage	
Germany	
Neomycin	5mg. Apply 2–4 times/day
Nebacitin ointment	
	2–4 times/ day

For eye infections (conjunctivitis)

Dosage	
England	
Chloramphenicol ointment	

Dosage	
France	
Collyre Chloramphénicol	

Dosage	
Germany	
Paraxin Augensalbe	

Antiseptics

See also: Sterilization

Antiseptics are chemical agents which *inhibit* the growth and development of micro-organisms, but do not necessarily kill them.

NOTE:

In emergencies, such as a liferaft situation, urine may be used.

Disinfectants kill the bacteria.

Antiseptics

England

Hydrogen Peroxide
Mercurochrome
Alcohol

France

Eau Oxygenée
Mercurochrome
Alcohol

Germany

Wasserstoff peroxid
Mercurochrom
Alkohol

Disinfectants

England

Tincture of iodine
Diluted bleach, 1 teaspoon per litre

France

Teinture d'iode
Eau de javel diluée, 1 teaspoon per litre

Germany

Merfen*
Bleichlauge, 1 teaspoon per litre

*Tincture of iodine is not sold in Germany.

Appendicitis

Symptoms

A dull pain* which begins in the central abdomen, and after a few hours moves to the lower right-hand quarter, becoming localized, sharper, more severe, and causing spasms of the overlying muscles.

Vomiting may occur.

The breath is foul.

Later, the stomach wall becomes hard and tender to the touch.

A moderate fever.

*NOTE:

Other possible causes of a dull pain

Food poisoning: pain is less well defined, and accompanied by more vomiting and diarrhoea.

Constipation: Pain is sharp, comes and goes and produces no muscle spasms or fever.

Swollen abdominal glands: pain is less precise, and without muscle spasms.

Usually occurs in younger people following a sore throat.

Treatment

The *only* certain treatment is surgery.

Until then, the person should be put to bed, given no food or purgatives, but allowed occasional sips of water.

Administer *only* a 'moderate' painkiller. A narcotic will tend to cause intestinal spasms. **See: Pain-killers**

If a fever and malaise develop, take Ampicillin. **See: Antibiotics**

Peritonitis, that is, the inflammation of the appendix, rarely occurs within eight hours of the onset, but if untreated by surgery is fatal.

Explanation

Appendicitis is an inflammation of a blind sac which leads from the beginning of the large bowel. The difficulty in recognizing it is that the position of the sac may vary, thereby changing the site of the pain.

Artificial respiration

If the person is not breathing

Begin artificial respiration *at once* ■ 39.

Tilt the head backwards, press down on the forehead, and push the lower jaw upwards by pressing the jaw bone below the ear.

Clear the mouth and throat of any foreign matter.

Seal your lips around the person's mouth, hold his nose closed with your fingers and forceably blow air into his mouth.

After each breath remove your mouth in order to allow the person to breathe out normally.

Inflate the lungs 3–5 times, then watch for chest movement.

If the air passages are not clear

Roll the person on to his side and deliver a sharp blow between the shoulder blades.

Maintain a steady rhythm of 10–12 breaths per minute.

If there is no movement of the person's chest

and

His colour is deathly blue-grey.

The pupils of his eyes are dilated.

No pulse can be felt.

The heart has stopped.

Immediately try to revive it

Turn the person on to his back.

Hit the chest smartly over the lower part of the breast bone.

If the heart does not begin to beat

Kneel beside the person, *begin heart compression*.

Place the heel of one hand on the lower end of the breast bone, the other hand on top of it, and press down firmly and evenly by rocking forward with your arms straight.

For adults – once a second.
Children – 80 times a minute.
Babies – 100 times a minute.

Avoid a jerky action.

If alone

Alternate artificial respiration with heart compression – one deep inflation of the lungs, then five heart compressions.

If two people

One person does the artificial respiration, the other the heart compression with a rhythm of one inflation to five heart compressions.

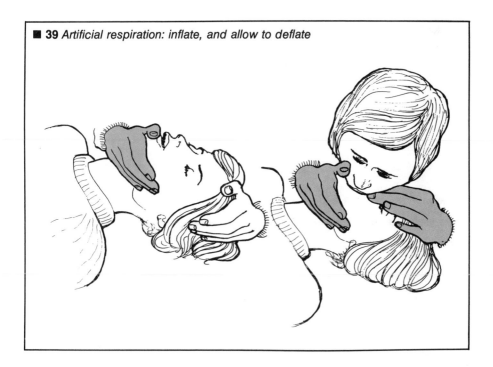

■ **39** *Artificial respiration: inflate, and allow to deflate*

B

Backstay

See: Rigging failures

Baggywrinkle

See also: Chafe, Sail repair

Materials

For one metre of baggywrinkle – about three metres of 3.5–4cm. old rope.

Two lengths of strong twine.

Procedure

Unlay the rope and cut it into 10cm strands.

Tie two lengths of twine in a vertical position between two fittings.

Take a strand of rope, hold it crossways, bring the ends up outside the twine, then pass them inside ■ 40.

Slide the strand up firmly against the knot.

Take the next strand . . . and so on.

Press the strands tightly against each other and knot the twine to hold them in place.

Unhitch the twine ■ 41.

Tape the sections of shroud where the baggywrinkle is lashed so it will not slip down ■ 42.

NOTE:

Instant baggywrinkle can be fabricated from paint rollers.

■ 40 *Baggywrinkle*　　■ 41

■ 42

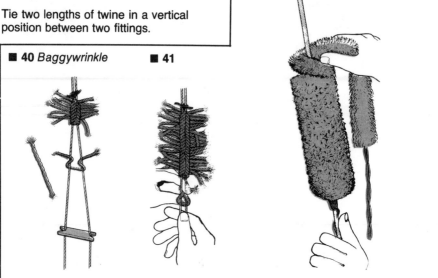

Bare poles	Beaching
See: Running	See: Aground

Barometer	Beacons
See: Weather forecast	See: Lights

Beaufort wind scale

Beaufort Number.	† Limits of Wind Speed in knots.	Descriptive Terms.	Sea Criterion.	Probable Height of Waves in metres *	Probable Maximum Wave Height in metres *
0	Less than 1	Calm	Sea like a mirror	—	—
1	1—3	Light air	Ripples with the appearance of scales are formed but without foam crests.	—	—
2	4—6	Light breeze	Small wavelets, still short but more pronounced. Crests have a glassy appearance and do not break.	0·15	0·30
3	7—10	Gentle breeze	Large wavelets. Crests begin to break. Foam of glassy appearance. Perhaps scattered white horses.	0·60	1·0
4	11—16	Moderate breeze	Small waves, becoming longer: fairly frequent horses.	1·0	1·50
5	17—21	Fresh breeze	Moderate waves, taking a more pronounced long form; many white horses are formed. (Chance of some spray).	1.80	2·50
6	22—27	Strong breeze	Large waves begin to form; the white foam crests are more extensive everywhere. (probably some spray).	3·0	4·0
7	28—33	Near gale	Sea heaps up and white foam from breaking waves begins to be blown in streaks along the direction of the wind.	4·0	6·0
8	34—40	Gale	Moderately high waves of greater length; edges of crests begin to break into spindrift. The foam is blown in well-marked streaks along the direction of the wind.	5.50	7·50
9	41—47	Strong gale	High waves. Dense streaks of foam along the direction of the wind. Crests of waves begin to topple, tumble and roll over. Spray may affect visibility.	7·0	9·75
10	48—55	Storm	Very high waves with long overhanging crests. The resulting foam in great patches is blown in dense white streaks along the direction of the wind. On the whole the surface of the sea takes a white appearance. The tumbling of the sea becomes heavy and shocklike. Visibility affected.	9·0	12·50
11	56—63	Violent storm	Exceptionally high waves. (Small and medium-sized ships might be for a time lost to view behind the waves). The sea is completely covered with long white patches of foam lying along the direction of the wind. Everywhere the edges of the wave crests are blown into froth. Visibility affected.	11·30	16·0
12	64+	Hurricane	The air is filled with foam and spray. Sea completely white with driving spray; visibility very seriously affected.	13·70	—

A Knot is one nautical mile per hour

† Measured at a height of 10 m. above sea level.

Berthing

Alongside pilings and uneven walls

An old plank or the gangway can be tied across two or more fenders ■ **43. See: Fenders**

The fenders can be strung on a line horizontally like sausages ■ **44**.

Three or more fenders can be tied together to form a fat one ■ **45**.

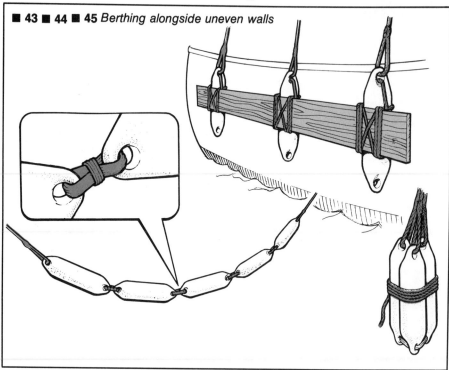

■ **43** ■ **44** ■ **45** *Berthing alongside uneven walls*

Alongside, without touching the quay

A kedge anchor can be laid out abeam.

If the boat is moored with springs, the warp can be attached at bow or stern ■ **46**.

The warp can also be passed under the keel to the other side, giving the kedge more scope and holding power. ■ **47. See: Careening**

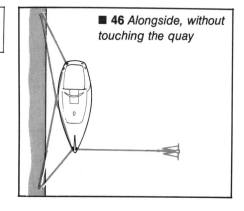

■ **46** *Alongside, without touching the quay*

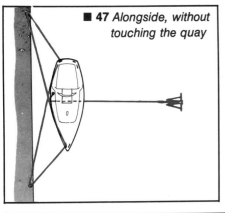

■ 47 *Alongside, without touching the quay*

WARNING:

Use chafing gear along the toe-rail. **See: Chafe**

Also beware of chafe against the keel **■ 48**.

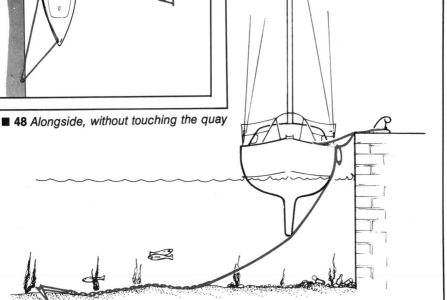

■ 48 *Alongside, without touching the quay*

Stern-to

Instead of dropping anchor and manoeuvring in reverse

Approach the quay bows-on **■ 49A**.

Attach a line from the bow to the quay **■ 49B**.

Back the boat out **■ 49C**.

Turn, then drop an anchor from the bow. Pass the warp attached to the quay to the stern **■ 49D**.

While paying out the anchor cable, warp the boat into her berth at the quay.

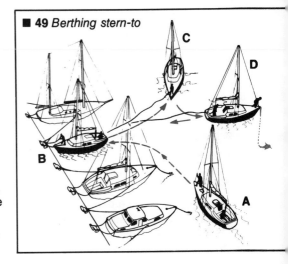

■ 49 *Berthing stern-to*

Bilge pump	Bleeding
See: Holes	See: Haemorrhages

Birds

See: Landfall signs, Liferaft

Block and tackle

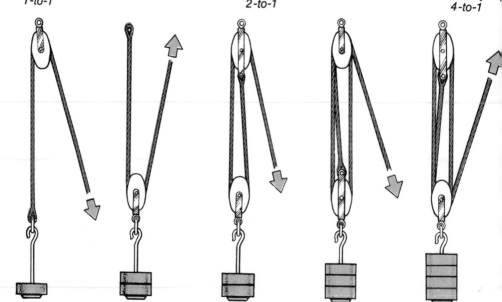

■ **50** *Single whip: 1-to-1* ■ **51** *Runner: 2-to-1* ■ **52** *Double-whip: 2-to-1* ■ **53** *Jigger: 3-to-1* ■ **54** *Handybill 4-to-1*

Booms

See also: Dismasted, Rigging failures

Broken

METHOD 1

Oars, floorboards, or boat-hooks can be used as splints, and the two broken pieces lashed together.

METHOD 2

The boom can be removed entirely and the mainsail set loose footed, but since the sail is no longer sheeted to the boom, more than likely the clew will need to be reinforced. **See: Sail repair**

Mainsails with reef points

Remove the boom and reef the sail until the foot is about the same length as an oar, jib boom, or spinnaker pole.

Loosely tie one end of the pole to the mast ■ **55A**.

Then, *either* lash the sail to the pole through the reef points ■ **55B** *or* tie it to the pole with the reefing line ■ **55C**.

Attach the mainsheet directly to the end of the jury-rigged boom. ■ **55D** The advantage of this method is that it removes strain from the mainsail clew.

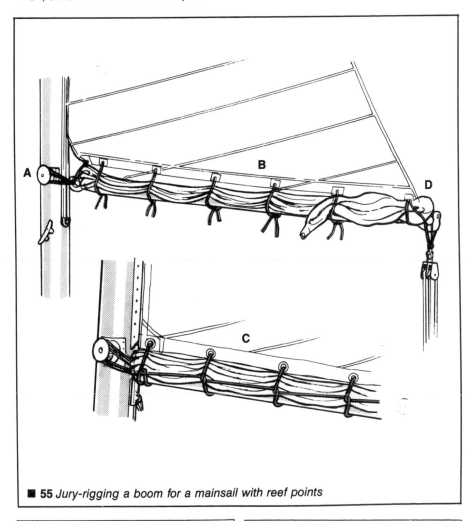

■ 55 *Jury-rigging a boom for a mainsail with reef points*

Bosun's chair	**Bottle screws**
See: Climbing the mast	**See: Rigging failures**

Bowline

See also: Knots

One-handed

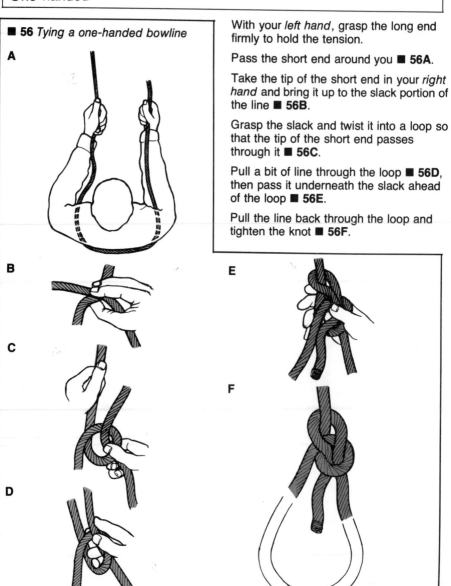

■ **56** *Tying a one-handed bowline*

A

B

C

D

E

F

With your *left hand*, grasp the long end firmly to hold the tension.

Pass the short end around you ■ **56A**.

Take the tip of the short end in your *right hand* and bring it up to the slack portion of the line ■ **56B**.

Grasp the slack and twist it into a loop so that the tip of the short end passes through it ■ **56C**.

Pull a bit of line through the loop ■ **56D**, then pass it underneath the slack ahead of the loop ■ **56E**.

Pull the line back through the loop and tighten the knot ■ **56F**.

Broaching-to

See: Heavy weather

Broken bones

See: Fractures

Bulldog clamps

See also: Dismasting, Rigging failures

Procedure

Bulldog clamps should be used in groups of 3 ■ **57**.

One clamp should be placed close to the eye ■ **57A**.

The two other clamps can be spaced 5–8 centimetres apart ■ **57B**.

The block of the clamp must be against the standing part of the rigging, or the longer section of wire ■ **57C**. This will ensure a strength of approximately 85–90% of that of the wire. If the clamps are placed the wrong way around the strength drops to about 75%.

Burns

Treatment

For minor burns

Leave the wound open.

Or coat completely with:
Plastic skin.
Plain soap dissolved in a little water.
A paste of bicarbonate of soda and water.

To lessen pain and help prevent blisters, immediately soak the wound in cold or iced water for 15–30 minutes.

NOTE:

If possible, do *not* break blisters as they

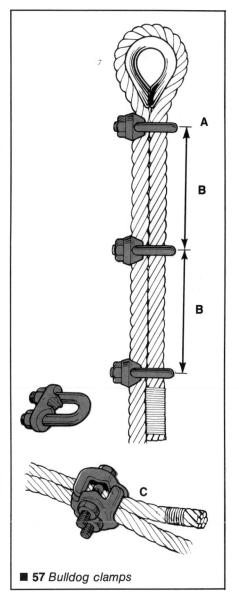

■ **57** *Bulldog clamps*

are a natural sterile covering until new skin forms underneath. If blisters must be broken, do so along the edge with a sterile needle, and then wash the wound with antiseptic or antiseptic cream. **See: Antiseptic.** Do *not* remove the blistered skin.

Rope burns

If the skin is *not* broken – pour cold water over the area for 5–10 minutes. Do not cover it.

If the skin is broken, cover with a non-adhesive dressing.

Burned mouth

Suck on a piece of ice, or wash the mouth with cold water.

The pain of a burned mouth can often be lessened by slowly drinking some cream or by sucking on some butter.

For major burns (more than 10% of the body)

Cleanse the burned areas thoroughly with soap and water.

Do *not* put on oils, salves or ointments.

Leave the wound open,

or

Apply a sterile Petrolatum dressing.

Victim should be kept warm.

Give the victim plenty of warm, salty fluids – for example: a mixture of $\frac{1}{2}$ teaspoon salt, $\frac{1}{2}$ teaspoon bicarbonate of soda, and 1 litre of water and orange juice – for palatability and potassium.

See: Pain-killers, Shock

C

Careening

Light displacement craft can usually be heeled over to expose nearly their entire keel; heavier craft to within a foot or two of the keel. For this reason careening is an excellent technique for:

Emergency hull repair.

Rudder repairs.

Seacock repairs.

Changing anodes.

Cleaning and painting the bottom.

METHOD 1 Careening from off the quay ■ 58

Prerequisites

A quay and calm water.

Strong anchors and chain.

Chafing gear. **See: Chafe**

A strong block and tackle of at least 4 to 1. **See: Block and tackle**

Procedure

Remove as much weight as possible from the boat. To lessen the strain on the mast internal ballast can be shifted to the side nearest the quay.

Also remove such items as batteries which could be damaged when the boat is heeled over.

Close all seacocks, portholes, cockpit lockers, sink drains and companion ways.

Seal the fuel tanks to prevent overflow.

Move the boat off the quay to a distance about $\frac{3}{4}$ the height of the mast.

Moor the boat fore and aft.

Lay out an anchor – or two – abeam, allowing plenty of scope. Pass the cable under the keel, secure it with chafing gear amidships, then lash it round the mast.

Secure the block and tackle at the hounds.

Slowly heel the boat over.

WARNING:

When heeled over, wooden boats may tend to leak through their topsides if they have not been sailed frequently.

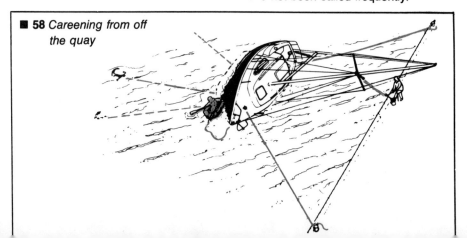

■ 58 *Careening from off the quay*

METHOD 2   Careening alongside the quay ■ 59

Prerequisites

A quay and calm weather

At least 5 car tyres

A large strong plank

A heavy car or truck

Procedure

Slacken the boat's mooring lines, fore and aft.

Lash the car tyres together, and secure them to the quay so that they hang into the water.

Secure the plank in place between the hull and the tyres.

Take a heavy warp, pass a bight around the mast, then hoist it to the hounds with the main halyard. Tie the other end to a strong point on the car or truck.

While heeling the boat slowly, watch the rigging and lifelines in order that they do not come in contact with the quay.

NOTE:

For light displacement boats it may be possible to lash securely the fall of the main halyard and carry the other end directly to the car.

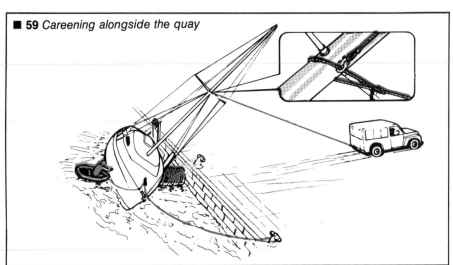

■ 59 *Careening alongside the quay*

Chafe

On lines at dockside

Cover the bights with plastic hose ■ 60.

Wind lengths of old rope around them ■ 61.

For quick protection, swathe the rope with old rags ■ 62.

Use bights of chain.

For protection of a bight slide a length of plastic tubing over the rope, then splice in an eye. A second piece of hose or tubing can be added and left so that it can be adjusted ■ 63. Old hose which is rigid is often preferable. It will hold the bight open, allowing mooring lines to be thrown easily over pilings or bollards.

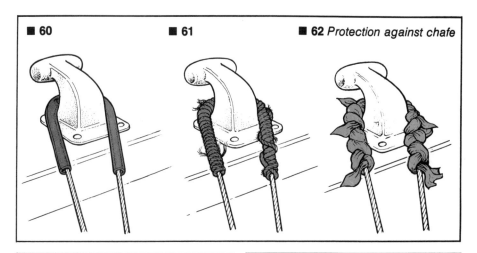

■ **60**

■ **61**

■ **62** *Protection against chafe*

If the chafed line must pass through a block

Cut a length of light canvas into strips 2–3cm. wide.

Wrap them around the line against the lay and secure them in place with twine, following the lay of the line. If tightly bound, this will only slightly increase the diameter ■ **64**.

If a line, passing through a block, is in danger of being chafed

Make a series of whippings covering the area of possible chafe.

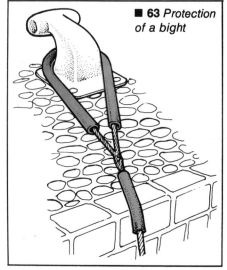

■ **63** *Protection of a bight*

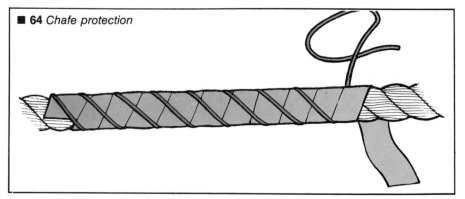

■ **64** *Chafe protection*

To prevent a tangle in case chafe occurs

Make short whippings every 10 centimetres ■ **65**.

An advantage of this method is that should the line chafe through, it will not jam the block.

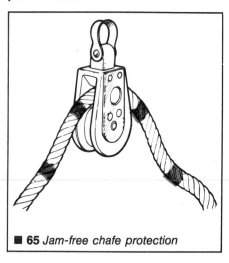

■ **65** *Jam-free chafe protection*

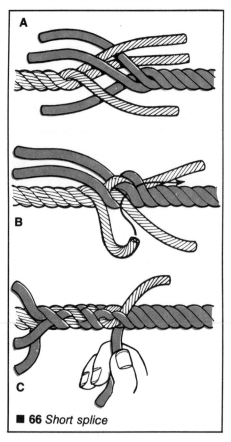

■ **66** *Short splice*

If the line is badly chafed

Short splice ■ 66

Cut the line and rejoin the ends with a short splice. This will restore about 95% of the original strength.

Long splice ■ 67

Cut the line and rejoin the ends with a long splice. This will restore 60% of the original strength, but its advantage is that the line's diameter is only slightly increased, hence it will pass through a block.

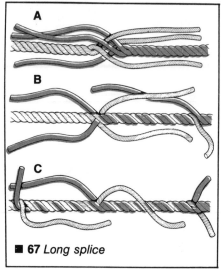

■ **67** *Long splice*

Whipping ■ 68

Cut the line. Tightly whip each end, then sew them together with strong twine and bind the whippings. This method should not be used for load-bearing lines.

■ **68** *Joining lines by whippings*

Sheetbend ■ 69

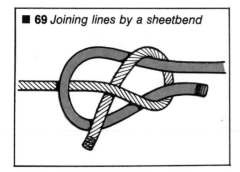

■ **69** *Joining lines by a sheetbend*

Bowline ■ 70

Cut the line, and rejoin the ends using two bowlines. This will restore about 50% of the original strength, so should not be used for load-bearing lines.

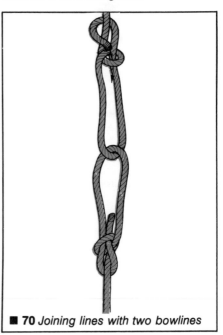

■ **70** *Joining lines with two bowlines*

For chafe on sails
See: Baggywrinkle, Sail repair

Climbing the mast

When climbing the mast

Always wear a safety harness.

Remain fully dressed.

Wear full-fingered gloves when ascending or descending, but not woollen ones, as they will tend to slip.

Wear sea boots, as they will grip the mast more firmly than shoes.

At night

Tape a torch to your forearm, so you have two hands free.

In heavy weather
Do *not* heave-to. If possible, sail with the wind abeam. When aloft, roll is easier to cope with than pitch.

Secure a downhaul to the bosun's chair.

Wear a lifejacket for protection in case you swing into the mast.

Attach a short length of line and a snap hook to the chair to secure yourself aloft.

If no bosun's chair is on board, one may be improvised from:

A tubular fender ■ **71.**

A boarding ladder ■ **72.**

A bowline on the bight ■ **73.**

If no winch is available

Attach one halyard to the bosun's chair.

Tie the end of a *second* halyard into a loop, which can be used as a stirrup.

While the climber supports himself on the stirrup, the bosun's chair is hoisted half a metre at a time.

Then climber transfers his weight to the chair, in order that the stirrup can be raised another half a metre.●

NOTE:

This method is slow, safe, and requires little physical effort of the person on deck.

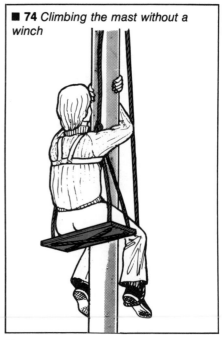

■ **74** *Climbing the mast without a winch*

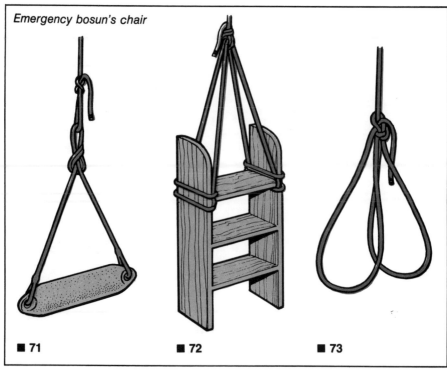

Emergency bosun's chair

■ 71   ■ 72   ■ 73

To make a ladder

METHOD 1 ■ 75, 76

Lay a length of stiff rope, such as a warp, on the deck, and at one foot intervals, tie large overhand knots to form stirrup-like bights.

Hoist the chain of loops aloft on a halyard, twist it several times around the mast to prevent it from swinging, then secure it tightly to a pin or cleat.

NOTE:

If the ladder is not long enough, the climber can secure himself to the cross-trees. The ladder can be unwound, hoisted to the masthead, then re-spiralled for the next stage of the climb.

METHOD 2 ■ 77

Lay a length of line on the deck – about three times the height of the ladder required – double it, then tie sheepshanks to form the steps.

Hoist the ladder aloft on a halyard and secure the end to the base of the mast.

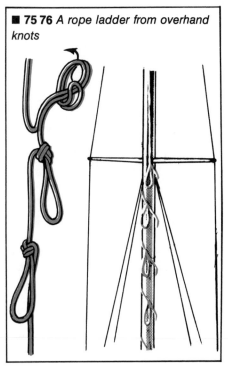

■ **75 76** *A rope ladder from overhand knots*

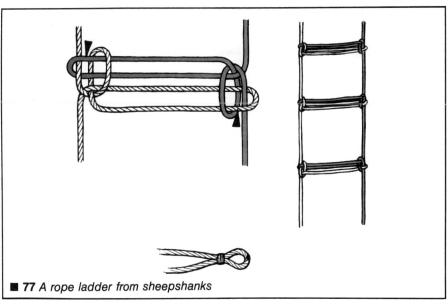

■ **77** *A rope ladder from sheepshanks*

METHOD 3 ■ 78

Using lengths of heavy cord, attach temporary ratlines to the shrouds with stopper knots (Rolling hitches). **See: Knots**

With a little practice, these knots can be tied with one hand, leaving the other free to hang on with. If the lengths of cord are pre-cut, they can be tied in place, one by one, as an ascent is made.

On an average-sized yacht, 8–12 lines should be enough to reach the cross-trees. Above that, if necessary, a web of ratlines can be tied between the upper shrouds, the mast and/or the forestay.

NOTE:

If the knots are being tied on stainless steel wire, a few turns of tape just below each knot will help it gain purchase.

METHOD 4 ■ 79

Short lengths of wood, for example cut from a boat hook, are tied with marlin spike hitches between two spare sheets to form a Jacob's ladder.

The ladder is tied to the main halyard, hoisted aloft, then cleated securely to the base of the mast.

METHOD 5 ■ 80

If the sail slides and their lashings are sufficiently strong, the mainsail can be slightly lowered and the slack in the sail used as ladder steps.

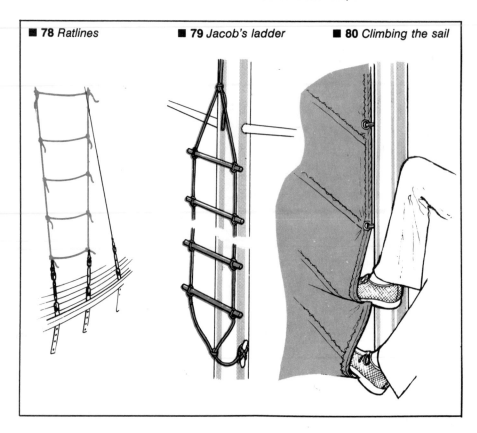

■ 78 *Ratlines*   **■ 79** *Jacob's ladder*   **■ 80** *Climbing the sail*

For single-handers

Make up a long block and tackle – two or three lines. **See: Block and tackle**

To go to the cross-trees with a mechanical advantage of 3:1 you will need at least four times the height.

Hoist one end of the block and tackle to the masthead or cross-trees. Since the lines tend to twist, and friction eats up the advantage, this method works best if there is a swivel at the upper block.

Attach the other end of the block and tackle to a bosun's chair, and haul yourself aloft.

Clouds

See: Weather forecast

Coach-roof repair

See: Deck-house repair

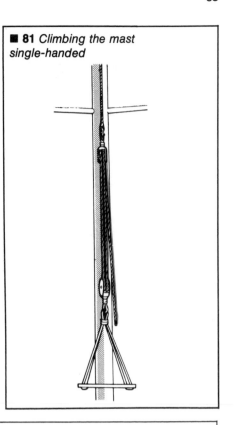

■ **81** *Climbing the mast single-handed*

Collision

See also: Accidents

If you think you are on a collision course with another vessel

Take an accurate bearing.

Wait, then take another bearing.

If the bearing remains constant, *you are on a collision course!*

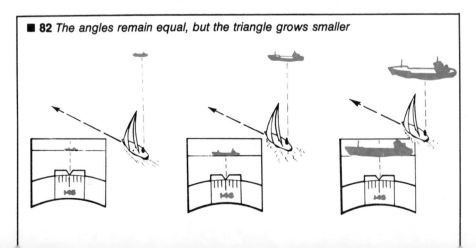

■ **82** *The angles remain equal, but the triangle grows smaller*

Avoiding action

Make all manoeuvres boldly and decisively so that the other ship will clearly understand your intentions.

If you suspect the other vessel has not seen you:

By day

Sound the appropriate warning signal of five or more short blasts on the horn.

By night

Flash the appropriate warning signal of five flashes or a morse 'U'.

or

Shine a strong torch up to the sails or let off a white flare.

NOTE:

A white flare does *not* indicate distress.
See: Flares

If there is a choice between changing course and changing speed, *change course.*

When changing course

Make the change a large one.

Change from one fixed course to another fixed course.

It is always safer to pass astern of another vessel.

If under sail, one must give way to

Other sailing boats which are on the same tack to leeward.

Other sailing boats on the opposite and starboard tack.

A vessel engaged in fishing.

A vessel navigating in a Traffic Separation Lane.

A vessel hampered by her draft such as a bulk carrier or supertanker.

A vessel restricted in her ability to manoeuvre such as a dredger or vessel laying a buoy.

A vessel not under command.

WARNING:

When avoiding fishing boats try to allow at least 150 metres for their nets.

If under power one must also give way to

A vessel under sail unless being overtaken.

A vessel on the starboard side.

NOTE:

If there is a risk of a *head-on collision*, both vessels alter course to starboard.

If a collision is inevitable

Attempt to turn on to the same course as the other vessel.

Attempt not to be struck directly abeam.

If you have the right of way, and the other vessel is to port, turn to starboard if possible.

Warning signals

NOTE:

If the signals are made by light, the *duration* of each flash should be about *one second*, the *interval* between flashes about *one second*, and the *interval between signals* at least *10 seconds*.

If the signals are made by sound, the *duration* of each short blast should be about *one second*, a long blast, *4–6 seconds*.

'I AM ALTERING MY COURSE TO STARBOARD.'

'I AM ALTERING MY COURSE TO PORT.'

'I AM GOING ASTERN.'

'LOOK OUT!' or 'I AM IN DOUBT REGARDING YOUR INTENTIONS.'

In a narrow channel or fairway

Warning signal (When approaching a bend or obstruction)

'I WISH TO OVERTAKE ON YOUR STARBOARD SIDE.'

'I WISH TO OVERTAKE ON YOUR PORT SIDE.'

'I AGREE TO YOUR WISH TO OVERTAKE ME.'

Collision mat

See: Holes

Constipation

Treatment

Plenty of fluids – preferably hot – fresh fruit, vegetables, and exercise should provide the solution.

If not:

Mild laxatives are: bran, garlic, wheat germ, brown rice, raisins and other dried fruits.

Strong laxatives are: boiled coffee, Epsom salts, three tablespoons of either olive or corn oil.

Explanation

Constipation is usually caused by a change in diet or environment, hence it often accompanies the beginning of a voyage. When the body adjusts to a new routine, regularity usually returns. Two or three days without a bowel movement will not do the body any harm. The record is over 100 days!

Medication

	Dosage
England Dulcolax*	10mg.

	Dosage
France Dulcolax*	10mg.

	Dosage
Germany Dulcolax*	10mg.

*Will require 6–12 hours for evacuation. If possible, take before going to bed.

For chronic constipation: Take an enema of one litre fresh water and one tablespoon washing-up liquid.

Cyclones

See: Law of storms

D

Danger

International Code of Signals

'U'
UNIFORM

'YOU ARE RUNNING INTO DANGER!'

Red **White**

■ 83

'PS' (Often used by light vessels)

'YOU SHOULD NOT COME ANY CLOSER.'

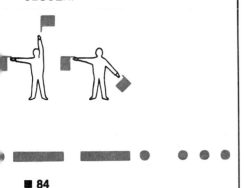

■ 84

Damage control gear

See: Holes

Date

If the date is unknown

Nearly all radio stations broadcast the date at either midnight or 0100 hours.

NOTE:

Should the announcement be in a foreign language, it is often easier to record the broadcast on a tape recorder, and decipher it later. For the numbers in eight languages, **See: Numbers**

The date by moon sight

Prerequisites

A sextant.

The Nautical Almanac.

The Time (G.M.T.)

Sight Reduction Tables.

Your approximate position, *plus or minus* one degree of latitude and/or longitude.

The approximate date, *plus or minus* 2–3 days.

Principle

The moon's place in the heavens changes dramatically from one day to the next, often passing through 12 degrees of

Hour Angle (celestial longitude) and several degrees of Declination (celestial latitude) in 24 hours. The sun, by contrast, changes its Hour Angle and Declination gradually, only a few minutes a day. Hence a moon sight calculated with the Hour Angle and Declination of the *wrong date* will yield an imposssible position line, one that is hundreds of miles from your approximate position. The position closest to your estimate position is the one with the correct date.

Procedure

Take a moon sight during either the day or night.

Using the Hour Angle and Declination of three or four consecutive days, work out the position lines in the usual manner. It will *not* be necessary to make the 'v' and 'd' corrections, as rough calculations will be sufficient.

Plot all the lines and label them by date.

All but one should be impossible. If not, or in doubt, wait until the moon is in another quadrant and repeat the process.

Death

Signs of death

No pulse or heart beat.

The pupils of the eyes are fixed and dilated.

No reaction to painful stimuli, for example, when jabbed with a pin or needle.

No fogging of a mirror held close to the nostrils or mouth.

Decreased body temperature.

Blue marks on those parts of the body on which the dead person has been lying.

After 2–3 hours joints become difficult to move.

Deck-house repair

Storm or wave damage

For cracks, broken deck joints and plank separations, the area to be re-inforced is at deck level.

Shoring can be cut from dinghy oars, spars, or boat-hooks.

Padding can be cut from floorboards, locker doors, or bulkheads.

Wedges can be cut from paint brush handles, cutting boards, or tools – such as chisels, screwdrivers, etc.

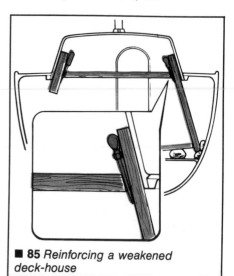

■ 85 *Reinforcing a weakened deck-house*

Demasted

See: Dismasted

Diarrhoea

Treatment

No food for 24 hours.

If the person is not vomiting, sufficient

liquids to prevent dehydration, for example, boiled skimmed milk, tea, barley water, or clear broths.

No alcohol or coffee.

Only 'mild' medication for the first 24 hours.

If diarrhoea continues, or is severe, stronger medication should be considered.

Medication

Mild: cooked, unseasoned white rice, carrot soup, yogurt, crushed bananas, cheese, apple juice and apple sauce.

Strong:

	Dosage
England	
Lomotil	1–2 tablets/ 4hrs.

	Dosage
France	
Diarsed	1–2 tablets/ 4hrs.

	Dosage
Germany	
Imodium	2 tablets/ 6hrs.

Complications

Diarrhoea can signal the beginning of a serious illness, such as Typhoid Fever or Dysentry, **See: Antibiotics,** hence the patient should be watched carefully.

Diarrhoea can be even more dangerous to small children as they can become dehydrated more quickly than adults.

Explanation

The two common causes of diarrhoea are:

1 – consuming bad food or drink, such as unripe or over-ripe fruit, bad tinned foods, inferior wine or beer, or impure water.

2 – food contaminated by bacteria, such as that badly cleaned or prepared, kept too long, or left in reach of flies or other insects.

If the cause has been unwholesome food or drink, the symptoms should lessen noticeably after six hours.

Diesel engine

See: Engine failure – Diesel

Disabled

See also: Distress signals

International Code of Signals

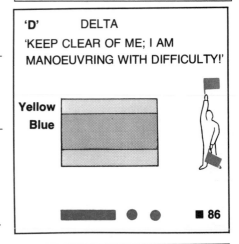

'D'   DELTA

'KEEP CLEAR OF ME; I AM MANOEUVRING WITH DIFFICULTY!'

Yellow
Blue

■ 86

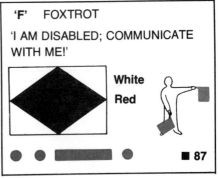

'F'   FOXTROT

'I AM DISABLED; COMMUNICATE WITH ME!'

White
Red

■ 87

Dismasted

See also: Jury-rigging, Rigging failures

If the mast, or any part of it goes overboard, the *immediate danger is*

The mast will stave in the hull.

or

The tangled rigging and sail will act as a sea anchor and drag the weather rail into the water.

Depending on sea and weather conditions

Hoist the broken mast on board.

Bring the mast alongside and lash it to the hull.

Salvage boom, sail, and rigging.

Tow the mast at a safe distance from the boat.

Lie to it as a sea anchor from the bow or stern.

Clear the deck

First, attempt to open the bottlescrews or remove the rigging pins.

Cut through any bronze bottlescrews as they are softer than rigging wire.

Cut through galvanized wire stays with sheers, croppers, abrasive wheel, hacksaw, or hammer and chisel against a metal block.

See: Rigging failures

Cut the stainless steel wire with bolt cutters or a hammer and chisel against a metal block.

> If the broken mast cannot be hoisted on board by hand

METHOD 1 ■ 88

A line is run through a block on the mast stump and then to the halyard winch.

■ 88 *Hoisting the mast on board with the mast stump*

METHOD 2 ■ 89

A spinnaker pole or jib boom is lashed to the mast and braced by a stanchion to serve as a crane arm.

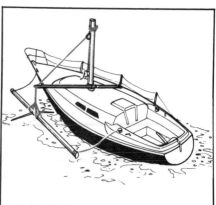

■ 89 *Hoisting the mast on board with the spinnaker pole*

METHOD 3 ■ 90

If the boat has two masts, the mizzen boom is run out abeam and used as a crane arm.

■ **90** *Hoisting the mast on board with the mizzen*

If the mast cannot be hoisted on board

It should be lashed alongside, well out of the water.

Put out all fenders. For emergency fenders **See: Fenders**

Run a line from the mast, through a block on the pushpit to the cockpit winch and raise the mast out of the water.

Lash the mast tightly to the hull using as many lines as possible ■ **91**.

WARNING:

Any spars or fittings which could endanger the hull should be cut away.

■ **91** *Lashing the mast alongside*

If the mast cannot be brought alongside

It must be towed at a safe distance from the boat ■ 92.

For towing gear **See: Towing**

■ **92** *Towing a broken mast*

If only the upper section of the mast is broken, but still on board

Do not try to cut off the downcoming part.

Secure it from the masthead to the stayed portion of the mast or a deck fitting ■ 93.

A block and tackle will probably be necessary ■ **94**.

If the lower portion of the mast is bent or broken, but still on board

Lash the two sections together ■ 93.

Lash the broken piece to another part of

the boat so that the two portions of the mast become a strong triangle ■ 95.

■ **93** *Securing a broken mast* ■ **94** *Securing a broken mast* ■ **95**

Distance at sea

For a person on deck, about two metres above the water

A rough guide is:

Distance – 4 miles

To shore
Objects, such as trees and houses are recognizable, but only in form. The beach is not visible.

To ships at sea
The superstructure of large ships can be seen. A yacht is a white spot.

Distance – 3 miles

To shore
Roofs and chimneys can be determined. Heavy surf can be seen.

To ships at sea
Freighter markings and bow waves are visible.

Distance – 2 miles

To shore
Windows and doors can be distinguished. But people are still invisible.

To ships at sea
Large buoys are barely discernible. At night, ship's sidelights come into view.

Distance – 1 mile

To shore
Details appear on buildings. Traffic can be seen and people are dots.

To ships at sea
Smaller buoys become visible, and freighter portholes.

Distance – ½ mile

To shore
People are moving lines, cars are identifiable.

To ships at sea
Sailors can be seen on deck. Rigging can be discerned.

Distance-off

METHOD 1   Vertical Sextant Angle ■ 96

Sight an object on shore, such as a lighthouse, whose height is known or can be estimated, and measure its angle above sea level. No allowance need be made for the height of the eye above the water (the Dip) or the state of the tide, as the result is an approximation.

Select the column in the Table which is closest to the height of the object. Read down to find your Sextant Angle, interpolate if necessary, then read off the distance on the vertical scale.

NOTE:

The heights of lighthouses are given to the centre of their lanterns not to the top of their structures.

Distance-off in miles	Height of the object ashore in metres				
	12	15	21	30	40
½	45′	57′	1° 19′	1° 53′	2° 27′
1	23′	28′	40′	57′	1° 14′
2	11′	14′	20′	28′	37′
3	8′	9′	13′	19′	24′
4	—	—	10′	14′	18′
5	—	—	—	11′	15′

■ 96 *Measuring the distance-off by a vertical Sextant Angle*

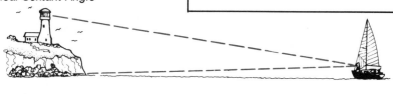

METHOD 2 A Four-Point (45°) Bearing ■ 97

Take a bearing on any stationary object which is 45 degrees off the bow.

With a log or speedometer, measure the distance between that point, A, and a second one, B, when the object, C, is directly abeam at 90 degrees.

Make allowances for tide and current.

At that moment the two sides of the triangle are equal, AB=BC. The distance travelled from point A to point B equals the distance from point B to the object at C.

METHOD 3 Doubling the angle on the bow ■ 98

Take a bearing from point A to any stationary object, C, which is *more than* 20 degrees off the bow.

With a log or speedometer measure the distance between that point, A, and a second one, B, when the angle off the bow is exactly double.

Make allowances for tide and current.

At that moment the two sides of the triangle are equal, AB=BC, but *not* necessarily joined by a right angle. The distance travelled from A to B then equals the distance from B to the object at C.

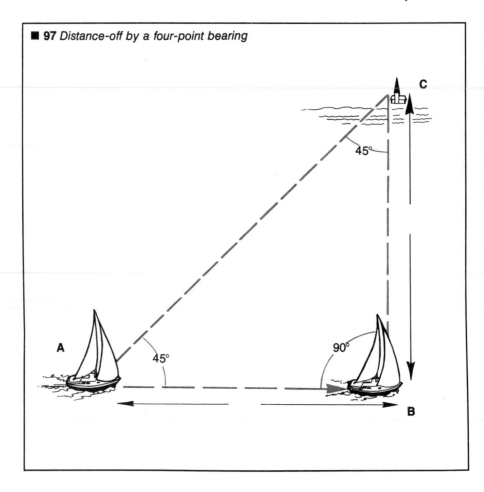

■ 97 *Distance-off by a four-point bearing*

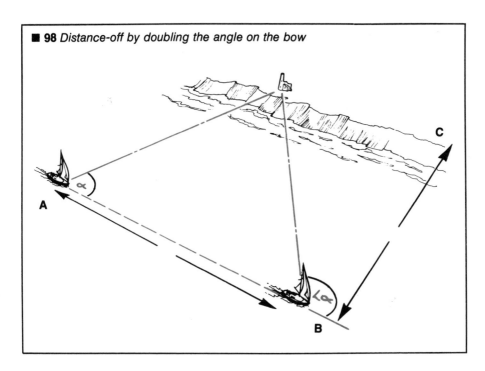

■ **98** *Distance-off by doubling the angle on the bow*

A

B

C

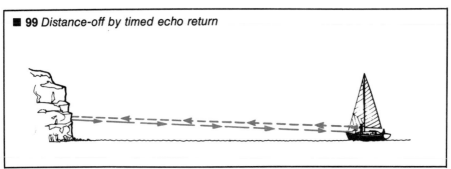

■ **99** *Distance-off by timed echo return*

METHOD 4 Distance by timed echo return ■ 99

In foggy weather a reliable estimate of the distance-off can be obtained by timing the echo of a gun or horn. The number of seconds from firing to the return of the echo times 0.09 will equal the distance in nautical miles to the point of echo return.

D = Distance-off in nautical miles

TER = timed echo return in seconds

D = TER × 0.09

Natural hand angles ■ 100, 101

When the arm is outstretched, the hand in a fist and the thumb extended, sighting across the knuckles produces an angle of approximately 10 degrees. Sighting over the tip of the thumb gives an angle of about 15 degrees.

When the hand is held flat, fingers and thumb spread wide, the basic angles of a right triangle can be roughly estimated. To sight with these angles the hand must be held close to the face with the eye at the base of the triangle.

0°
15°
30°
45°
90°

10°
15°

■ **100** *Natural hand angles*

■ **101** *Natural hand angles*

Distillation

See also: Solar still, Water

Materials

A stove.

A large pot.

A metal funnel (plastic will probably melt).

A length of pipe or tubing. In emergencies, this can be taken from the engine or the boat's water system.

Some cloth, rags or a towel.

Procedure ■ 102

Cover the pot with the funnel and attach the tubing to the small end.

Wrap the cloth or rags around the tubing.

Fill the pot with salt water and place it on the stove. As the water boils, pour cool seawater over the rags or cloth.

■ **102** *Fresh water by distillation*

Principle

When the water boils, the steam rises into the funnel and the tubing where it is condensed by contact with the cool metal. The 'fresh' water drips out the end of the tube.

NOTE:

If the water still tastes salty, repeat the distillation process a second time.

Distress signals

See also: Danger, Disabled, Help!, Medical assistance

A gun

A shot or other explosive signal fired at intervals of about a minute.

A fog-signalling apparatus

A continuous sounding.

Rockets or shells throwing red stars

Fired one at a time at short intervals.

SOS · · · – – – · · ·

Sent out by radiotelegraphy or any other signalling means.

MAYDAY

Sent out by radiotelephony or any other means.

Broadcasting the spoken word.
MAYDAY, MAYDAY, MAYDAY, – Boat's name 3 times – MAYDAY, MAYDAY, MAYDAY, – Ship's position – MAYDAY, MAYDAY, MAYDAY

FLAGS

International Code Signal of Distress:

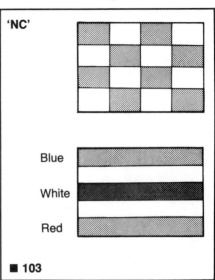

'NC'

Blue
White
Red

■ 103

or

Flying the national ensign upside down.

or

A square flag having above or below it a ball, or anything resembling a ball.

Flames

Burning oily rags in a bucket.

Rags or any rubber material can be tied to a boat-hook or oar, soaked in diesel or paraffin, lighted, and held outboard.

Red flares

Either parachute flares or hand-held.

A smoke signal giving off orange-coloured smoke

A dye marker

When released it will spread a coloured stain on the water.

An emergency position indicating radio beacon

A hand signal

Slowly and repeatedly raising and lowering arms outstretched to each side.

Other distress signals on small craft

The ensign hoisted upside down.

The ensign made fast high in the rigging.

Rags or clothing tied to a raised oar.

Acknowledgement of a distress signal

By day

An orange smoke signal.

Three white stars – possibly accompanied by bangs (thunderflashes) – fired at one minute intervals.

By night

Three, single, white star rockets at one minute intervals.

By aircraft

By day

Rocking its wings from side to side.

By night

A series of green flashes with a signal lamp.

If the message is received but not understood

By day

The aircraft will make a complete circle in a clockwise direction.

By night

A series of red flashes with a signal lamp.

Diving signals

International Code of Signals

'A'

ALPHA

'I HAVE A DIVER DOWN.'

'KEEP WELL CLEAR AND AT A SLOW SPEED.'

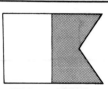

White   Blue

For the diver   'I AM O.K.'   'I NEED ASSISTANCE.'

■ 104

Docking See: Berthing	**Drogue** See: Sea anchors
Doctor See: Medical emergencies	**Drowning** See: Artificial respiration

Drying out

See also: Aground

Alongside

While the boat is fully afloat, slacken the mooring lines and heel the boat against the quay. A 10 degree list should be enough ■ 107.

Methods to heel the boat ■ 106

A line from the hounds can be taken to a strong point ashore.

Attach one end of a warp to a snatch block or bight riding on a lower shroud or taut halyard. Attach the other end to a strong point ashore. In this manner a constant tension is maintained as the boat rises and falls.

Lay the anchor and chain along the quayside deck.

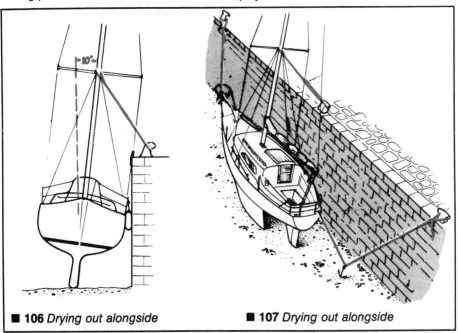

■ 106 *Drying out alongside*   ■ 107 *Drying out alongside*

Weights, such as anchors, can be shackled on to the mooring lines to keep a constant quayside pull.

An inflatable can be placed on the deck and filled with water.

See: Careening

WARNING:

Before the boat dries out, if possible check the bottom for rocks or other obstacles.

Be ready to unshackle the upper shroud and attach chafing gear in case it touches the quay ■ **107**.

On board boats with short keels keep movement to a minimum, as they can easily tip forward.

Drying out heeled over ■ 108

Heel the boat towards the high side of the bank, most likely the shoreward side. This will probably mean heeling in the *opposite* direction from when trying to break free. **See: Aground** for different methods of heeling the boat.

Move or secure any items such as batteries, lockers, or galley equipment which might be damaged when the boat is laid over.

Seal the fuel and water tanks.

Pump the bilges while the boat is still upright.

Close the portholes, cockpit lockers and sink drains.

■ **108** *Protecting the hull as she dries out*

As the water recedes, check the bottom for obstacles.

Protect the vulnerable parts of the hull with fenders, mattresses, sails or an inflatable. Lay floorboards or spars against any obstacles such as rocks or stones.

At low water, lay out a strong anchor in the direction of deep water so that when the tide rises the boat can be hauled free.

WARNING:

Do not heel bilge keel hulls, but for stability pivot them so the bow or stern points up the bank.

NOTE:

If the boat is lying on her beam ends, she must be made watertight. Tape all portholes and cockpit lockers closed. If the boat is lying towards the wind or in a downhill position, lash a sail or awning over the cockpit.

Makeshift legs ■ 110

These can be made from booms, spinnaker or jib poles or even driftwood.

Each leg must be well lashed to the chain plates, or failing those, the bottlescrews of the lower shrouds and the deck stanchions.

Each leg must be guyed fore and aft.

The two legs need to be lashed together with a cross bar which is also lashed to the mast.

Depending upon the character of the bottom, feet may be necessary. These can be made from metal jerry cans, floorboards, or locker doors. They can be slid under the legs as the boat dries out, or better still, they should be lashed to the legs.

NOTE:

Anchors should be laid out, fore and aft,

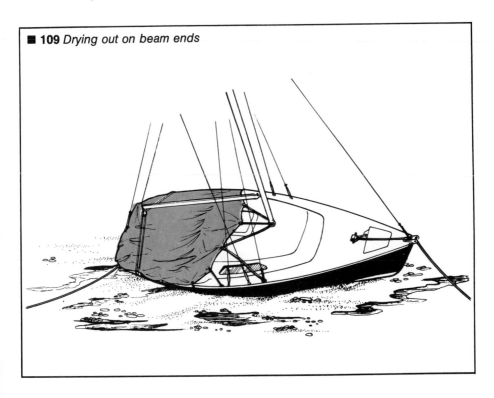

■ **109** *Drying out on beam ends*

to prevent the boat from ranging as the tide comes in.

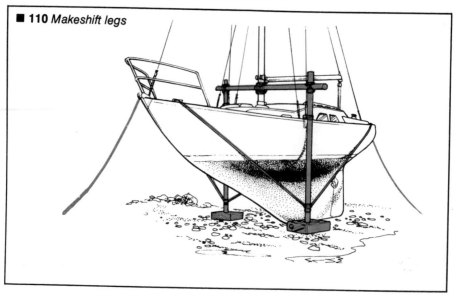

■ **110** *Makeshift legs*

An alarm system for grounding at night ■ 111, 112

Drop a weight attached to a line over the side until it hangs 10–20cm. below the keel.

Run the line through a block to the cockpit or skylight where the end secures a pot or pan in place ■ **112.**

When the weight touches ground, the line slackens and the pan crashes to the deck.

■ **111** *An alarm for grounding at night*

■ **112** *An alarm for grounding at night*

E

Ears

Water in the ear

Treatment

In most cases the water will drain by gravity when the person is lying on his side.

If not, gently work a piece of cotton wool into the ear with a twisting motion.

NOTE:

Do not put any sharp objects in the ear.

Pain

More than likely this is caused by an infection in the ear itself.

Treatment

A few drops of warmed, but not hot, olive oil can have a soothing effect.

Take antibiotics. **See: Antibiotics**

Foreign body in the ear

Pull the ear *up* and *back* which makes it possible to see far into the ear drum. If the object can be seen, remove it carefully with a pair of tweezers.

Insects in the ear

Put a drop or two of olive or cooking oil, alcohol, or spirits – rum or whisky – in the ear which should kill it. Then, remove carefully with tweezers.

Echo sounder

METHOD 1   Depth equals position
■ 113

If lost

While holding a steady course, make a series of soundings – at least a half dozen – at regular intervals, for example, every quarter- or half-hour, and record the distance travelled. Do not forget to correct all soundings for Tide. **See: NOTE** below

Plot the soundings on a sheet of tracing paper using the same scale as the chart. Then attempt to align the tracing over the chart until the line of soundings matches the soundings on the chart.

If sailing on a known course

Make a series of soundings – at least half a dozen – at regular intervals, and record the distance travelled. Do not forget to correct all soundings for Tide. **See: NOTE** below

Plot the soundings on a sheet of tracing paper using the same scale as the chart. Place the tracing over the chart and align it along your course. When the soundings are matched with those of the charted depths, the last sounding along the line becomes a 'fix' ■ 114.

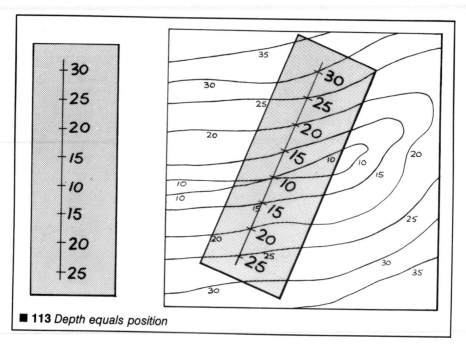

■ 113 *Depth equals position*

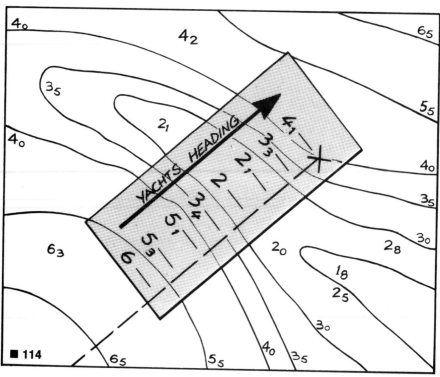

■ 114

METHOD 2 'Running Down' a fathom line (contour navigation) ■ 115

Once a charted fathom line (contour line) – corrected for Tide (**See: NOTE** below) – is crossed, its direction can be determined by making a series of short tacks. One can then 'run down' or follow the line in much the same manner as old captains once 'ran down' latitude lines to their destinations. In this case, however, the course tacks across the fathom line, thus maintaining contact and following it to a known point.

NOTE:

Before using an echo sounder reading for navigational calculations allowance must be made for:

1 – The distance from the transducer to the surface of the water.

2 – Tide.

In tidal waters, charted depths are for Mean Low-Water Springs, that is, the low water mark at Spring tides, which is *unlikely* to be the depth at the moment. New charts use L.A.T. – Lowest Astronomical Tide – which is generally lower than Mean Low-Water Springs. If the tidal range is known, this can be taken as an error factor.

or

If the tidal range and the time of tidal change is known, the approximate depth above chart datum can be calculated using the 'Law of Twelfths'.

The first hour tide rises or falls by one-twelfth of its range; the second, two-twelfths; the third, three-twelfths; the fourth, three-twelfths; the fifth, two-twelfths; the sixth, one-twelfth.

■ 115 *'Running Down' a fathom line*

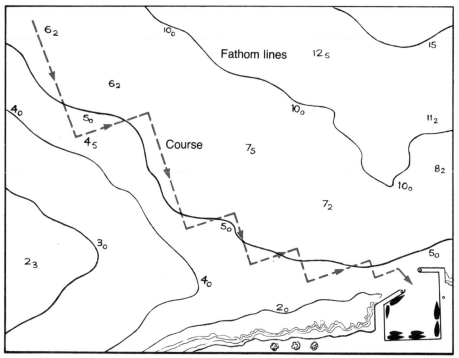

METHOD 3 Character of the bottom indicates position

Occasionally, knowing the character of the sea-bed can help establish one's position, or conversely, where one isn't!

Soft mud ■ 116

The leading edge of the display is not clearly defined. Once spurious echoes are eliminated, the Gain control will probably be set higher than for other bottoms, as soft mud is more absorbent of an ultrasonic pulse and usually returns a fairly weak echo.

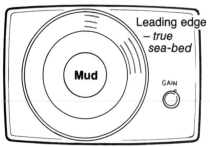

Zero flash

Leading edge – true sea-bed

Mud

GAIN

■ 116 Echo sounder display in soft mud

Sand or gravel ■ 117

The leading edge is strong and clearly defined, and does not alter with changes in the Gain control. A second, or sometimes even a third rebound echo may be visible.

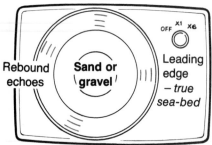

Zero flash

OFF X1 X6

Rebound echoes

Sand or gravel

Leading edge – true sea-bed

■ 117 Echo sounder display in sand or gravel

Rocks ■ 118

The echo is elongated and broken into segments even with a low setting of the Gain control. This is due to the multiple echoes which are returned from the uneven bottom surface. As the boat moves through the water, the leading edge should oscillate rapidly.

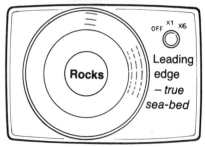

Zero flash

OFF X1 X6

Rocks

Leading edge – true sea-bed

■ 118 Echo sounder display with a rocky bottom

Engine failure

Diesel

WARNING:

An over-heated engine can quickly suffer damage. Turn it off immediately, and check:

The water inlet for blockage.

The cooling water level in the engine.

The oil level.

The fan belt to the water pump.

That the propeller is clear.

WARNING:

Any loss of oil pressure indicates a serious problem. Stop the engine. Check the oil level and refill if necessary. If there is still no pressure, let the motor cool. Then, if absolutely essential, such as berthing in port, run the engine for only very short periods of time.

WARNING:

If the oil is milky coloured and diluted with water, stop the engine. Check the oil level and refill if necessary. More than likely the head gasket is broken. This will not lower the oil pressure. Run the engine only at low revolutions.

If the engine does not start, but the starter motor turns over and the engine pre-heats

NOTE:

If the pre-heating indicator lamp burns brightly straight away after turning the switch, this usually indicates that the pre-heating spark plug is defective. The engine will not start until it is replaced.

Check and bleed the fuel system

Check the fuel filters for dirt, water and that they are full.

If the filters are not full

The tank is empty.

There is an air leak in the line, either between the tank and the filters or between the filters and the fuel pump.

Bleed the fuel filters

Open the valve on top, and wait (or pump, should there be a pump attached) till fuel runs out without air bubbles. Then close the valve securely.

Bleed the fuel pump

Open the valve on top, and pump until a steady, stream without bubbles comes out. Then close the valve securely.

Bleed the injectors

Open the lock-nuts 1–2 turns on the connection between the fuel pump and the injector ports. Turn over the engine. As soon as fuel comes out, tighten the lock nuts (the sequence is not important).

The engine may start after two or three injectors have been bled.

NOTE:

To be certain there is no petrol in a diesel oil tank, drain out a little fuel and place it in a saucer. If it disappears quickly it is petrol. Diesel oil evaporates very slowly.

NOTE:

If a head gasket has been ruptured, add cooling water constantly. The engine can be run at low revolutions. Do not stop it, otherwise it will not start.

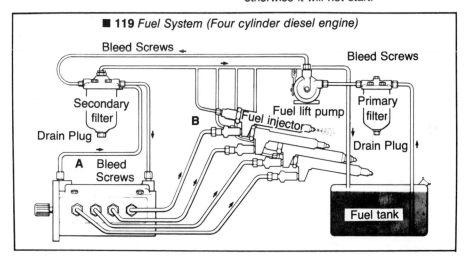

■ 119 *Fuel System (Four cylinder diesel engine)*

Petrol

WARNING:

An over-heated engine can quickly suffer damage. Turn it off immediately, and check:

The water inlet for blockage.

The cooling water level in the engine.

The oil level.

The fan belt to the water pump.

That the propeller is clear.

WARNING:

Any loss of oil pressure indicates a serious problem. Stop the engine. Check the oil level and refill if necessary. If there is still no pressure, let the motor cool. Then, if absolutely essential, such as berthing in port, run the engine for only very short periods of time.

WARNING:

If the oil is milky coloured and diluted with water, stop the engine. Check the oil level and refill if necessary. More than likely the head gasket is broken. This will not lower the oil pressure. Run the engine only at low revolutions.

When a petrol engine suddenly stops

With noise

More than likely there is serious damage – a broken timing chain, piston, valve, etc.

Without noise

The fault is probably electrical.

When a petrol engine stops with a splutter

The fault is probably in the fuel system.

If the engine does not start

Checking the electrical system

1 — If the starter motor does not turn over more than likely:

The battery is dead.

The battery is not properly grounded (earthed).

One of the connections in the battery – ignition switch – starter motor circuit is bad.

2 — If the starter motor turns over

check the electrical connections between:

The spark plugs and the distributor head ■ **120A.**

The distributor and the coil ■ **120B.**

The coil and the distributor base ■ **120C.**

The coil and the ignition switch.

The ignition switch and the battery.

The battery and the ground (earth).

Sandpaper away any oxidation and tighten any loose nuts.

3 — If the engine still does not start

Disconnect the wire which runs from the coil to the centre of the distributor at the distributor head and hold it close – about two mm. – from the motor block, and turn over the engine. If there is a good spark, the next thing to check is the spark plugs.

Remove the spark plug, lay it on the block and check for a spark.

Are the spark plugs wet?

Is the gap correct – usually between 0.6 and 0.9mm.

If in doubt, change the plugs or pre-heat them with a candle or lighter.

If there is no spark, open the distributor and check the rotor for corrosion and the centre connection in the distributor head. Check the distance between the points with a feeler gauge – roughly 0.4mm.

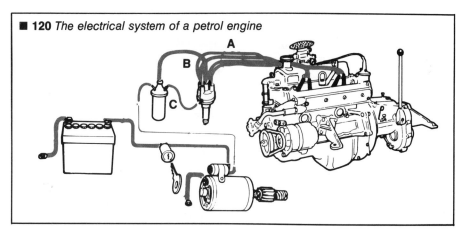

■ **120** *The electrical system of a petrol engine*

If there is still no spark, either the coil or the condenser is defective.

NOTE:

If the engine has not been run for a long time, and will not start, it is better to check the fuel system before the electrical system.

Checking the fuel system

1 – Unscrew the fuel line to the carburettor, and turn over the engine ■ **121A.**

If fuel comes out:

The carburettor is defective.
Dismantle and clean it.

If no fuel comes out:

The fuel tank is empty.

The fuel pump is broken.

There is a leak or blockage in the line.

2 – Disconnect the intake to the fuel pump ■ **121B.**

If the fuel pump is lower than the tank and no fuel appears:

The tank is empty.

There is a leak or blockage in the line.

Suck on the line if the fuel pump is higher than the tank, and if no fuel appears:

The tank is empty.

There is a leak or blockage in the line.

If the fuel appears at the fuel pump intake:

The fuel pump is probably either broken or blocked.

Dismantle and clean it.

NOTE:

Water in the fuel tank

Small quantities of water can be burned off by mixing $\frac{1}{2}$ litre of alcohol to every 200 litres of fuel. The water will combine with the alcohol and be burned off in combustion.

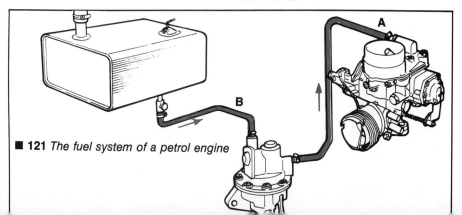

■ **121** *The fuel system of a petrol engine*

Evacuation

See also: Abandon ship!, Distress signals

Yacht to helicopter

Procedure

Make the transfer from a dinghy or liferaft towed astern

or

Keep the boat on a predictable course.

Make the transfer from the stern.

If possible, release the backstay, and support the mast with halyards or the topping lift. **See: Rigging failure**

Show a green light when you are ready to make the transfer, a red one if you are not ready.

If a litter or basket is lowered do not touch it until it makes contact with the deck as it may be charged with static electricity.

WARNING:

Do not make fast the line or wire lowered from the helicopter.

If a sick person is being transferred alone, a note explaining his condition, treatment, and any medication he has been given should accompany him. His hands and arms should be well secured to the litter.

NOTE:

If a harness is not lowered, use a bosun's chair. For emergency bousun's chairs **See: Climbing the mast**

Yacht to ship

Procedure

Approach the ship on its leeward side.

If the ship has pumped out oil.

Attempt to stay in the slick.

Slacken the upper shrouds and lifelines.

Put out all fenders. For make-shift fenders **See: Fenders**

If a stretcher is passed from the ship

Stand off.

Secure the sick person to the stretcher, then come alongside again for the transfer.

If no stretcher is available

One may be constructed from a pipe cot, sail bags lashed to dinghy oars, or a mattress supported by oars or boat-hooks.

WARNING:

Be prepared to lose your mast. Take down all sail, and, if possible, remove the boom and secure it on deck.

Explosion

See: Fire

Exposure

See also: Frostbite, Drowning

Treatment

If legs or feet appear to be insensitive or 'asleep'

See: Immersion foot

If frozen white spots appear on the body

See: Frostbite

Put the survivor in a *tub* of warm water, preferably about 37°C.

Slowly add hot water – about 42°C.

Keep the legs out of the water so that the body will warm up first.

If no tub is available

Lay the survivor on his back, fully clothed,

and slowly and carefully pour warm water over him.

If no hot water is available

Remove the survivor's clothes, and cover him with a blanket, pre-heated if possible.

Serve him hot drinks with plenty of sugar.

If necessary, warm the survivor with your own body, and massage him gently.

NOTE:

Do *not* give alcohol to anyone suffering from exposure.

Eyes

Foreign body in the eye

Do *not* rub the eye!

Wash hands thoroughly before touching the eye.

Treatment

Examine the lower lid first.

If the object is there, bring the upper lid down over the lower lid, which may dislodge the object.

If this does not work, wash the eye with fresh water in an eye cup or a clean drinking glass. Hold the cup firmly against the face, tilt the head back, and roll the eye several times.

If the object is lodged on the upper lid, the lid should be inverted over a pencil or matchstick. Remove the object with shred of clean, moistened cotton wool on the end of a toothpick.

If the object is lodged on the cornea, or if it cannot be seen, close the eye, cover with a patch of cotton or gauze and anchor shut with a piece of tape. Removal by the uninitiated can be dangerous.

If there is a suggestion of infection, treat with antibiotic ointment. **See: Antibiotics**

Chemicals in the eye

Wash the eye *continuously*, using large amounts of water. Pour the water from the inner to the outer part of the eye. Do this for several minutes. Then repeat after 15 minutes. A few drops of mineral, olive, or castor oil after copious washing will soothe any inflammation.

F

Fatigue

Symptoms

Lack of concentration.
Forgetfulness.
Simple 'stupid' errors.
Lack of efficiency.
Strange visual experiences, distortions or hallucinations.

Treatment

Plenty of warm clothing.

For immediate strength – sugar in the form of honey or sweets.

To prevent errors and ensure rational decisions, one should monitor one's behaviour by introspection, speaking out loud, or listing on paper carefully what is to be done next.

Medication

'Stay-Awake' pills*

	Dosage
England	
Dexamphetamine	
Sulfate	tablets 5mg.
	2 times/day

	Dosage
Germany	
Captagon	$\frac{1}{2}$–1 tablet/
	1–2 times/
	day

Amphetamines are nearly unobtainable in France

Fenders

In emergencies use ■ 122

Rubber tyres ■ 122A.

Lifejackets.

Pillows in sailbags ■ 122B.

Sealed detergent bottles or plastic water containers ■ 122C.

Cockpit cushions ■ 122D.

Mattresses.

NOTE:

For squeaky fenders, pour a little washing-up liquid over them. This will also form a protective film against oil and pollution in the water.

Home-made fenders ■ 123

Materials

Two metres heavy rope.

A piece of foam rubber such as that cut from a cushion or pillow.

One square metre of canvas.

Needle and thread.

Procedure

Knot the two ends of the rope and triple the loop ■ 123A.

Wrap the foam around it and bind it in place ■ 123B, 123C.

Cover with canvas. Sew the seams and the ends to the rope ■ 123D.

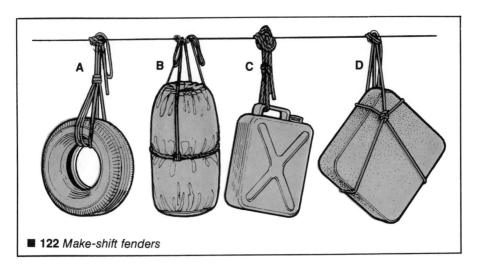

■ **122** *Make-shift fenders*

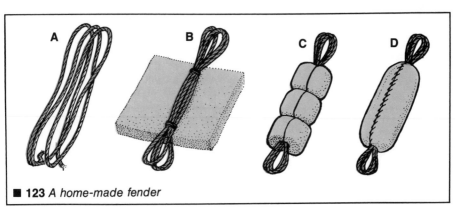

■ **123** *A home-made fender*

Ferrocement repair

Cracks

All breaks in the hull, even scratches, should be repaired immediately to prevent water from entering and rusting the mesh.

A patching putty can be made from epoxy, sand and water.

If rust stains have already appeared, the damaged area should be scraped back to the mesh before patching.

For superficial rust a wire brushing is sufficient.

Clean away loose concrete with a paint scraper or screwdriver.

Sand any exposed mesh.

Fill with the epoxy-sand putty.

Fibreglass repair

Cracks ■ 124, 125

If necessary, widen the crack so that it will hold a repair putty ■ 125.

Extend each end of the break about a centimetre to relieve any stress.

Clean away all dust.

Mix gelcoat, resin, hardener and loose bits of glass fibre mat into a paste or putty.

Fill the crack and press the putty in with a knife.

Leave some excess on top as the putty tends to shrink slightly when drying.

Cover the area with a plastic sheet and tape it down tightly since gelcoat will not cure properly if exposed to the air ■ 125.

NOTE:

When working with glass fibre one should *always* wear gloves.

Holes

METHOD 1   Temporary patching ■ 126

Make a patch from thin marine plywood, copper or tin sheeting, or metal from an unrolled tin, such as an oil or fruit can. Cut the patch so that it overlaps the hole by at least three fingers' width.

Drill holes in the patch first, then use it as a template to make holes in the hull. The holes should not be more than four fingers apart.

Use a thick coating of mastic for a gasket or, failing that, an old towel, sail cloth, or rags well greased with heavy lubricating grease or soaked in paint.

Bolt the patch in place, using plywood or pieces of metal as washers on the inside.

If the hole is bigger than fist-sized

An inside and outside patch will be necessary. In this case, the patches should be reinforced with a plank, then bolted to each other *through* the hole, which will also help to hold them rigid.

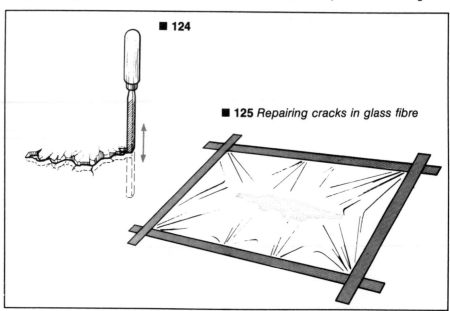

■ 124

■ 125 *Repairing cracks in glass fibre*

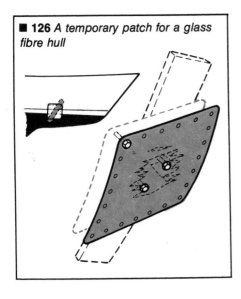

■ 126 *A temporary patch for a glass fibre hull*

Make a backing plate from metal sheeting, linoleum, or, if necessary, cardboard covered with cellophane. This plate should be at least 10cm. larger than the hole, and should be securely taped on the outside of the hull.

Cut the glass fibre cloth or mat to cover the hole and overlap at least 5cm. Different layers should be criss-crossed.

Saturate the glass fibre patch with resin-hardener mix and then lay it in place.

Remove all air bubbles as these could become weak points in the patch **■ 128C.**

NOTE:

Hardening time is dependent upon air temperature, the exact mix of hardener and resin and the thickness of the patch.

METHOD 2   A glass fibre patch

If possible, make the patch from the inside of the hull.

With a saw, cut away all of the damaged area, until only unfractured material is showing.

Round the hole, if possible **■ 127.**

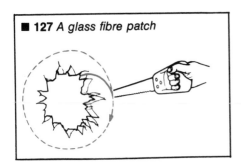

■ 127 *A glass fibre patch*

Bevel the edges inwards with a file **■ 128B.**

On the outside, sand the area 5–10cm. around the hole.

On the inside, sand the area 10–15cm. around the hole.

Dust the area well.

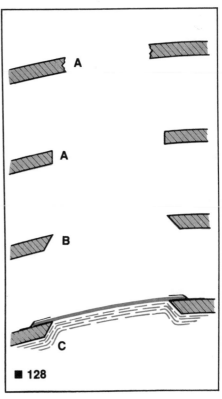

■ 128

Fire

See also: Abandon ship!, Evacuation, Distress signals

International Code of Signals

'J'

JULIET

'I AM ON FIRE AND HAVE DANGEROUS CARGO ON BOARD, KEEP WELL CLEAR OF ME!'

Blue
White
Blue

■ 129

In light winds

Drop all sails and stop the boat.

In strong winds

Sail downwind immediately. (The object being to minimize the apparent wind as quickly as possible.)

Fire-fighting

Wet your clothes.

Direct the fire extinguisher towards the base of the fire, not towards the flames.

Cushions and mattresses afire

They should be thrown overboard.

Glass fibre

Water should be used in conjunction with fire extinguishers to cool the material, as hot glass fibre can easily catch fire again.

Petrol and oil

Water will *not* extinguish the fire, but will help to cool the area and prevent the flames from spreading.

Engines

Throw a wet blanket or towel over it and attempt to suffocate the flames.

A person alight ■ 130

Throw him over the side.

or

Lay him on the deck.

Stand at his head holding a wet blanket or towel in front of you. Secure the corners with your feet, then fall forward over the burning man.

Never point a fire extinguisher at a person alight.

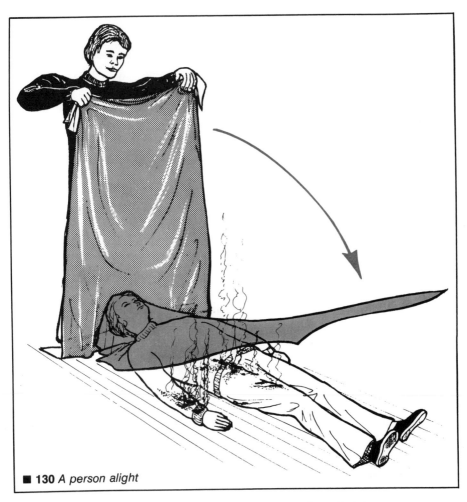

■ **130** *A person alight*

When opening a door

Crouch low, as the flames and heat will tend to rise. Also visibility is better near the deck ■ **131.**

When opening a hatch

Do so from the side with the hinges ■ **132.**

NOTE:

Those not involved in fire-fighting, should ready the dinghy and liferaft and leave the boat.

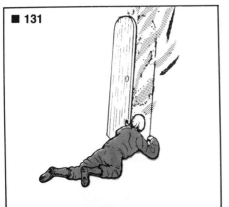

■ **131**

■ **132**

To take survivors from a burning boat

METHOD 1

Approach the boat bow to bow. This will lessen the impact should the fuel tanks explode. In general, the force of a boat tank explosion is directed upwards by the shape of the hull.

METHOD 2

Tow or drift a dinghy or inflated liferaft close to the other boat on a long line. Let the survivors climb on board, then haul them to you.

For treatment of burns. See: Burns

The fire-fighting principle

Three elements are necessary to support any fire:

Oxygen – Fuel – High temperature.

These can be thought of as constructing a fire triangle.

Eliminate any side, and the fire will go out.

Oxygen   Fuel

Fire

High temperature

Fish

See also: Fishing, Poisoned fish

Poisonous fish ■ 133, 134, 135, 136

In general, these species have proportionally large teeth or beaks as they often feed on coral. Hence, scavengers who feed on them may also be poisonous.

WARNING:

Do not eat any fish which puff up like balloons when caught.

■ **133** *Trigger fish*

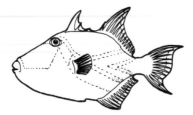

■ **134** *File fish*

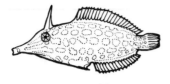

■ **135** *Puffer fish (uninflated)*

■ **136** *Puffer fish (inflated)*

Venomous fish ■ 137, 138, 139, 140, 141, 142

These fish can usually be identified by their spiny appearance. This often includes bristles and veil-like appendages.

If in doubt, do not touch or eat them.

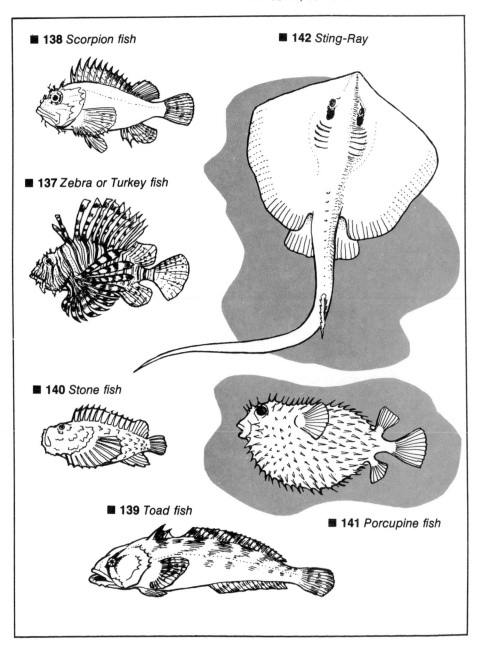

■ **138** *Scorpion fish*

■ **142** *Sting-Ray*

■ **137** *Zebra or Turkey fish*

■ **140** *Stone fish*

■ **139** *Toad fish*

■ **141** *Porcupine fish*

Fish hook injuries

Removing a fish hook from another person

METHOD 1 ■ 143

Place the hand on a hard surface, palm up.

Loop the line around the curve of the hook, and wind the ends several times around your forefinger.

With the other hand, grip the eye of the hook, and push it down to disengage the barb.

Align the string with the shank's long axis, and *yank hard*.

NOTE:

If necessary, the entire operation can be done one-handed.

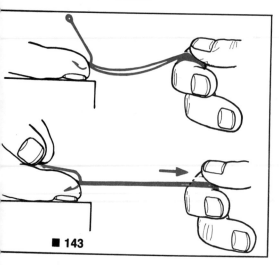

■ 143

METHOD 2 ■ 144

Insert a hypodermic needle along the barbed side of the hook, with the bevelled part of the point towards the inside of the hook's curve.

Pull gently on the shank to disengage the barb.

Then, push the needle gently downwards until its hole locks over the barb.

Rotate the hook shank slightly downwards and the hook curve upwards until the needle and hook are removed through the original wound.

METHOD 3 ■ 145

Cut off the eye of the hook with a pair of wire cutters.

Push the shaft *into* the flesh until the pointed, barbed end comes out of the skin.

Grip it firmly, then pull the shaft through the wound and out.

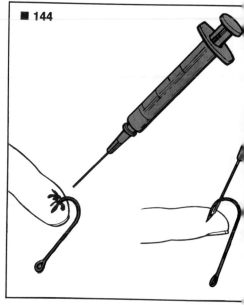

■ 144

Clean the wound thoroughly and cover with antiseptic. **See: Antiseptic**

If signs of infection appear – pain, redness and swelling. **See: Antibiotics**

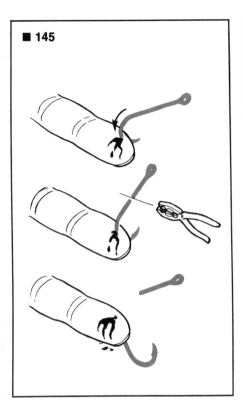

■ 145

Fishing

See also: Fish, Fish hook injuries, Poisoned Fish

Emergency fishing gear ■ 146, 147, 148, 149

Lures

These can be manufactured from unravelled pieces of rope, strips of plastic bag, silver paper, bright-coloured rags, feathers or the skin or entrails of a fish. If possible, a wire leader should be attached to the hook, and the lure constructed around it ■ 146, 147, 148.

A spinner can be fashioned from a tin or beer can. In this case, the hook must be screwed, bolted or wired to the pieces of metal ■ 149.

In general, yellow, white or silver lures are best early in the morning or at sunset, brightly coloured ones during the day.

Make-shift lure

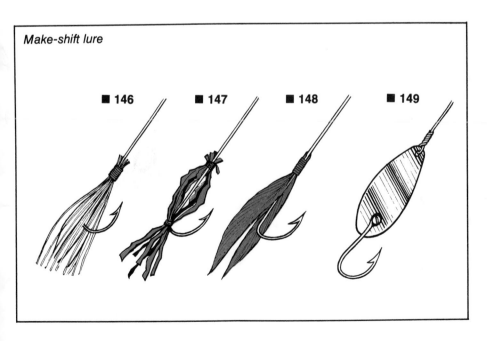

■ 146   ■ 147   ■ 148   ■ 149

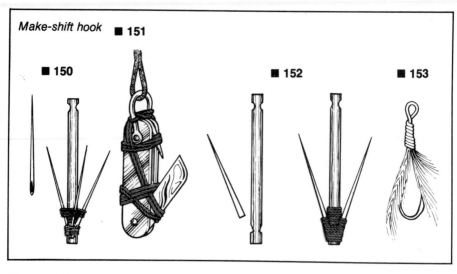

Make-shift hook ■ 151

■ 150   ■ 152   ■ 153

Hooks ■ 150, 151, 152, 153

These can be manufactured from such items as pins, knives, shoe nails, fish bones, pencil clips, tins or a bent fork.

Fishing knots ■ 154, 155

A single Cairnton knot.

Tying the line to a swivel.

After tying the half hitches pull the knot tight. It will draw up into a neat roll.

NOTE: ■ 156

Many survivors of liferaft ordeals report the most effective means of catching fish is to gaff or harpoon those beneath the raft. A harpoon can be fabricated by lashing a knife to the end of a paddle, and a gaff by lashing on a large fish hook.

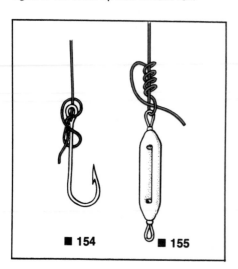

■ 154   ■ 155

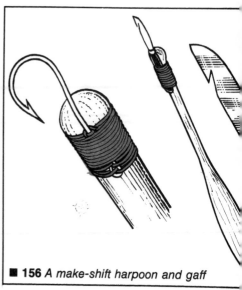

■ 156 *A make-shift harpoon and gaff*

Fishing line

Small lengths of moderately strong line can be improvised from shoe laces, strips of cloth, a belt, or woven from unravelled rope or fabric.

Fish trap ■ 157

This can be fabricated from a sea anchor, paddles and light clothing, or a bucket with holes in it.

NOTE:

Many types of fish are attracted to light, even of low intensity. On a moonlit night even a mirror reflecting the moonlight on the water can be effective.

Drying marine food

The flesh of most marine animals can be dried in the sun and, if kept dry, preserved for months.

When cut into strips of not more than 2cm. thickness, the meat should dry within four days. It can be eaten at any stage in the drying process.

For quicker drying, the meat can be shredded into small pieces, and then either laid on trays or hung on lengths of twine.

Drying fish

For small fish (those of less than two kilos) ■ 158

Chop off the heads and tails.

Clean.

Break the backbones so that the fish are flat.

Lay them in the sun, and sprinkle on some salt.

Then string the fish on a line between the shrouds until they become hard.

Store below, either in an open-weave basket or hanging between deck beams.

To use:

Soak the pieces in fresh water for a day, changing the water at least twice.

For larger fish

De-bone as much as possible.

Cut into strips or fillets.

Then, follow the same procedure as for smaller fish.

Drying shark meat

Cut the meat into fillets.

Soak in a strong brine solution for at least

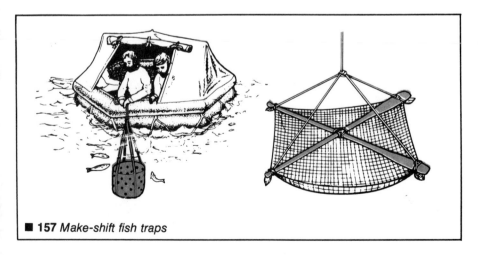

■ **157** *Make-shift fish traps*

a day, changing the water several times.

When the 'shark' smell is gone, hang up to dry in the same manner as any other fish.

Drying crab and lobster

Boil in seawater for 10 minutes.

Remove from the shell.

Shred the meat with your fingers, then lay it out in thin layers on trays or plates.

Place them in the sun, and turn the meat every hour or two. In two days the meat should be well dried and ready for storage.

Drying shrimp

Boil in seawater for 10 minutes.

Take off the shells and heads, and cut away the veins.

Arrange the meat on plates or trays.

Place them in the sun, and turn the meat every hour or two. In 3–4 days the meat should be well dried and ready for storage.

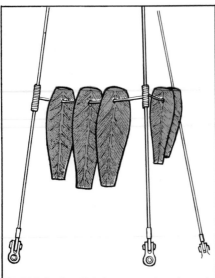

■ 158 *Drying fish between the shrouds*

Flares

See also: Distress signals

ORANGE SMOKE – Distress

RED – Distress

WHITE – Warning of imminent danger, such as collision

or

Acknowledgement of a distress signal

GREEN – Special signals, often used by the Navy and by searching aircraft

BLUE – Request for a pilot

Firing

Flares should be held at arm's-length, pointing away so that the dross does not drip on to hands or body.

For maximum effect, flares should be fired *downwind*.

Flares should be fired in groups of two, the second a minute or two after the first.

Range at night

A hand-held flare – about five miles.

A parachute flare – about 20–25 miles.

A star shell – about 10 miles.

Emergency flares

Oil-soaked rags burning in a bucket.

Burning plastic material, such as polystyrene and mattress and cushion stuffings.

WARNING:

As a general rule, flares have a three-year life span, if stored in dry conditions. The magnesium powder used in firing slowly deteriorates and beyond three years cannot be considered reliable.

Flooding

See: Holes

Fog

Warning signs

The air becomes extremely moist and clammy.

Brightwork, cabin windows and portholes steam with condensation.

Smoke tends to lay in the sky in long layered lines.

Lights take on a distinct halo effect.

Changes appear in the colour of the cloud base.

Principle

Sea fog is nothing more than a cloud resting on the surface of the water, which is formed by the meeting of cold air and warm water or the reverse. The most common type is *advection fog*, that is, the passage of a current of warm air over the colder surface of the sea. As the air is cooled, a temperature inversion takes place, and when the air is cooled below the dew point, condensation occurs and water vapour appears in the form of fog.

This kind of fog is quite common near coasts where a warm off-shore air current encounters a cooler sea. Should that air current be humid, often it creates a dense layer of fog on the sea, while four or five metres above it the warmer air is completely clear. In this kind of fog one encounters ships with the tops of their masts pointed into a clear sky and their decks a foggy gloom.

If in congested waters or shipping lanes

Lifejackets should be worn.

The liferaft straps should be unlashed.

A radar reflectors hoisted nou less than four meters above the deck. **See: Radar reflectors**

If conditions permit, the dinghy can be towed astern.

Visibility scale used in weather forecasts

	Visibility
Fog	Less than a 1000 metres
Mist (Humidity more than 95%)	1000 to 2000 metres
Haze (Humidity less than 95%)	1000 to 2000 metres
Poor	2000 metres to 2 nautical miles
Moderate	2–5.5 miles
Good	over 5 miles

Distances in fog

In dense fog, distances can be difficult to judge. Crumpling a sheet of newspaper into a ball, throwing it over the side, and watching it float out of sight will give some idea as to the limits of visibility. However, fog is seldom uniform in density. A horizon of 300 metres can double or triple, or half, from one moment to the next.

A look out should try vantage points as high and low as possible as in patches he may be able to see under or over the bank. If the fog is shallow, the first sighting of another vessel could be high in the air – a bridge or cross-trees appearing to float on a whispy cloud.

See: Distance at sea

Sound in fog

In foggy conditions, sounds are often deflected, diminished or amplified, even to such an extent that the ring of a buoy's bell can appear to grow weaker the closer one approaches to it, or the grunt of a diaphone seems to be nearer than a whistle when it is actually twice as far away. Also, it is quite possible to have one impression of direction and intensity on deck and another aloft.

There are no hard and fast rules.

A look out should always keep in mind the possibility, especially if the fog is light and patchy, that the lighthouse, lightship or buoy that he is straining to hear may be experiencing a completely clear day and thus not sending out a signal.

NOTE:

Lightships and lighthouses have their own distinctive signals which can be found in the *Admiralty List of Lights*.

Types and characteristics of fog signals

Type (Chart abbreviation given in brackets)

	Characteristic
Diaphone (Dia)	Strong note of low tone ending with easily distinguished grunt
Siren (Siren)	Medium powered high or low note or both together
Reed (Reed)	Lower powered than siren with high note. May be hand operated using little power
Tyfon (Tyfon)	Powerful medium pitched note similar to a ship's fog signal
Nautophone (Nauto)	High note similar to Reed
Electric fog horn (EF Horn)	Powerful medium pitched note. Several sound frequencies produced simultaneously
Gun (Gun)	Explosive signals from a gun. An Acetylene Gun gives a brilliant flash at the time of the explosion
Explosive (Explos)	Signals explode in mid-air. Usually placed in outlying positions
Bell (Bell)	wa=wave actuated. Notes may be of any pitch depending on size of bell
Whistle (Whis)	Usually placed on isolated buoys
Gong (Gong)	Occasionally used at pier ends etc.

Sound signals in restricted visibility

With a horn, siren or foghorn

●   'I AM TURNING TO STARBOARD.'

● ●   'I AM TURNING TO PORT.'

● ● ●   'I AM GOING ASTERN.'

● ● ● ● ●   'LOOK OUT!'
'I AM IN DOUBT REGARDING YOUR INTENTIONS.'

● ▬▬▬ ●   'WARNING! THERE IS A DANGER OF COLLISION.'
'Romeo'

Normally
The sounding of a bell indicates a vessel at anchor or aground

The sounding of a fog horn or whistle indicates a vessel underway

Vessels underway

Power vessel underway

▬▬ 2 minutes ▬▬ 2 minutes ▬▬

Power vessel underway – but stopped and making no way through the water

▬▬ ▬▬ 2 minutes ▬▬ ▬▬ 2 minutes ▬▬ ▬▬

Vessel fishing, towing, restricted in ability to manoeuvre, or a sailing boat on any tack

▬▬ ● ● 2 minutes ▬▬ ● ● 2 minutes ▬▬ ● ●

Last vessel in a tow

▬▬ ● ● ● 2 minutes ▬▬ ● ● ● 2 minutes ▬▬ ● ● ●

Pilot vessel making way

▬▬ ● ● ● ● 2 minutes ▬▬ ● ● ● ● 2 minutes
▬▬ ● ● ● ●

Pilot vessel stopped but not at anchor

▬▬ ▬▬ ● ● ● 2 minutes ▬▬ ▬▬ ● ● ●
2 minutes ▬▬ ▬▬ ● ● ●

Pilot vessel on duty

● ● ● ●

NOTE:

Fishing boats have no special anchor
signals in fog.

A vessel aground

The bell – and gong – signals are preceded and followed by three strokes of the bell.

 1 minute 1 minute

3 strokes   5 seconds   3 strokes

NOTE:

If the vessel aground is longer than 100 metres a gong is sounded rapidly for five seconds after the ringing of the bell.

Vessels at anchor

Ship at anchor

 1 minute 1 minute

5 seconds   5 seconds   5 seconds

Ship at anchor more than 100 metres in length

 1 minute 1 minute

5 seconds 5 seconds   5 seconds 5 seconds   5 seconds 5 seconds

Pilot ship at anchor

 1 minute 1 minute

5 seconds 4 short blasts   5 seconds 4 short blasts 5 seconds 4 short blasts

Oil rig at anchor

 30 seconds 30 seconds
'U'   'U'   'U'

Forestay

See: Rigging failures

Fractures

See also: Shock

Fracture of the extremities

Symptoms

Swelling of the limb.

The limb is out of alignment.

Intense pain.

Treatment

See: Shock

Immobilize the limb with a splint – sail batten, boat-hook, etc.

If the fracture is within the joint, immobilize the entire limb until proper medical help can be found.

Medication

See: Pain-killers and Tranquillizers

Skull fracture

Symptoms

A depressed area on the skull (which may be hidden by a bruise).

Blood or fluid draining from the nose, ears or mouth.

Difficulty swallowing.

The pupils of the eyes may be unequal in size.

Loss of consciousness.

Drowsiness.

Vomiting.

A change in behaviour.

NOTE:

Symptoms such as loss of consciousness, drowsiness and vomiting may appear up to 24 hours after the injury.

Treatment

Let the fluids continue to drain by putting the head forward. Take Ampicillin. **See: Antibiotics**

Clean the wound and stitch it if necessary. **See: Wounds**

Wrap the wound with a *loose*, fluffy dressing.

Keep the victim warm, quiet and immobilized until medical help can be found.

Medication

See: Pain-killers but do *not* use narcotics for a head injury.

See: Tranquillizers – administer only if absolutely necessary as they may mask the symptoms.

Fractures of the spine

Symptoms

Any injury to the back should be regarded as a possible fracture of the spine.

Paralysis.

A deformed spine.

NOTE:

If the person is unconscious, prick the toes or fingers. No reflex indicates paralysis.

Treatment

Immobilization – The person should be moved *only if absolutely necessary*, and then retaining *complete body alignment*. Even if the injury appears to be slight, movement should be restricted, as it may cause paralysis.

Frostbite

See also: Exposure

Symptoms

The frozen part will be white and numb.

NOTE:

Frostbite occurs most often on the nose, cheeks ears, toes and fingers.

Treatment

The frozen part should be thawed as quickly as possible by:

Immersing it in water which is at normal body temperature (about 37°C).

or

Wrapping it in warm blankets.

NOTE:

Massage should be avoided as it may damage tissue. Also, the frozen part *should not* be rubbed with snow or cold water as has been formerly advocated as an emergency treatment.

When the part thaws, it should be exercised.

Do not remove any dead tissue unless it is badly infected.

Blisters that form should not be disturbed.

No weight should be put on the injured part.

Take pain-killers as necessary. **See: Pain-killers**

For infection, take antibiotics. **See: Antibiotics**

G

Gale

See: Heavy weather

Grounding

See: Aground

Glass fibre repair

See: Fibreglass repair

GRP repair

See: Glass fibre repair

H

Haemorrhages

See also: Shock, wounds

To stop bleeding

Apply continuous pressure to the site.

Do this for at least 10 minutes in order to give the clot time to form, or longer if necessary.

If the bleeding is severe

Attempt to control it by pressing on a pressure point ■ **159.**

Apply a tourniquet as a last resort.

If the bleeding is pulsing:

An artery has been severed.

If the bleeding cannot be controlled by direct pressure:

Apply a tourniquet between the wound and the heart. Release it gradually for a few seconds as the bleeding stops.

If it doesn't stop bleeding.

The artery must be tied off. **See: wounds**

Should it be necessary to leave the tourniquet on, it must be released for a few seconds every 15 minutes – in cold weather, every 10 minutes.

NOTE:

If the person loses a large amount of blood, he may go into shock and require a transfusion. **See: Shock**

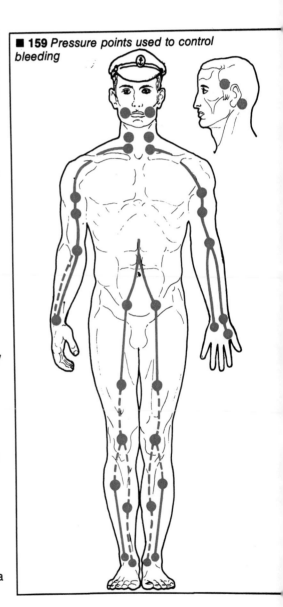

■ **159** *Pressure points used to control bleeding*

Heat exhaustion

See also: Sunstroke

Symptoms

Skin is pale and moist.

NOTE:

By contrast, in a condition of *Sunstroke* the skin is dry, flushed and hot.

Weakness.

Headache.

Often nausea and vomiting.

Treatment

Rest in a cool place.

The head should be lowered.

Drink plenty of fluids.

Take extra salt.

For a weak pulse – strong black coffee.

Heaving-to

Purpose

To cope with a storm by 'stopping' or retarding the movement of the boat.

As a general rule one should *Heave-to under sail* then, as conditions worsen – seas rise, wind gains force or the boat heels dangerously – either take down all sails and *Lie a-hull, Lie a-hull to a sea anchor*, or at that point decide to run with the storm. **See: Running**

For maximum 'stopping' power, such as may be necessary *on a lee shore: Ride to a sea anchor.*

WARNING:

Boats with long straight keels usually heave-to more easily than short fin keels. Some modern designs have great difficulty heaving-to under sail and may require someone at the helm or another tactic must be chosen.

Heaving-to under sail

See: Stormsails

The jib is backed, sheeted to windward.

A reefed mainsail or trysail is sheeted amidships.

The helm is lashed a-lee.

The force of the mainsail and the rudder is counterbalanced by the backed jib. When the bow comes up into the wind, the jib causes the boat to fall off. The rudder and mainsail drive the boat ahead, and the cycle is repeated ■ **160.**

WARNING:

Even hove-to under sail, the boat may easily make 1–2 knots headway.

NOTE:

When lashing the tiller use strong shock cords or elastic nylon line leaving the rudder a little play to prevent damage.

■ **160** *Heaving-to under sail*

Heaving-to under sail

Heaving-to under sail can usually be accomplished by any of several sail plans. Which one depends upon such factors as hull shape, windage, and rigging. The following combinations have been used successfully:

Sloops with a small fore-triangle

1 – A backed storm-jib and a reefed mainsail or trysail sheeted in ■ **162.**

2 – A backed storm staysail and a riding sail (a storm-jib hanked on the backstay and sheeted in) ■ **161.**

3 – Only a riding sail ■ **162.**

4 – Only a trysail.

Sloop with a large fore-triangle

1 – Only a backed jib ■ **163.**

2 – Only a riding sail.

3 – A backed storm staysail and a riding sail.

Traditional cutter

1 – A close-hauled storm-jib, backed staysail and a reefed mainsail ■ **164.**

2 – A backed spitfire jib and a storm trysail.

3 – A backed storm staysail and a storm trysail.

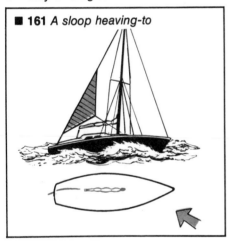

■ **161** *A sloop heaving-to*

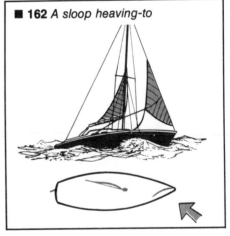

■ **162** *A sloop heaving-to*

■ **163** *A sloop heaving-to*

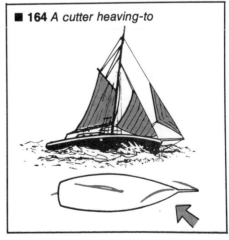

■ **164** *A cutter heaving-to*

Ketch

1 – Only a reefed mizzen.

2 – A backed jib and a reefed mizzen ■ 165.

3 – Only a storm trysail.

4 – A backed jib and a reefed mainsail.

Yawl

1 – Only a storm trysail ■ 166.

2 – A backed jib and the mizzen well sheeted in.

3 – Only a reefed mizzen.

4 – A backed jib and a reefed mainsail.

WARNING:

When heaving-to with only the mizzen and the helm lashed down, the boat should *not* lie too close to the wind. There is a danger of being thrown backwards by a wave and damaging the rudder.

Schooner

1 – Only a reefed fore-sail.

2 – A storm fore-staysail and a main stormsail or a reefed down mainsail ■ 167.

NOTE:

To find the correct rudder angle, some experimentation will be necessary.

■ **165** *A ketch heaving-to*

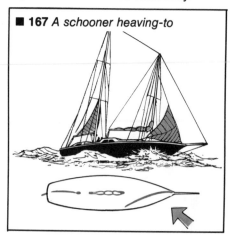

■ **167** *A schooner heaving-to*

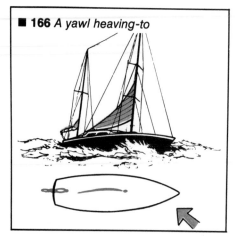

■ **166** *A yawl heaving-to*

Lying a-hull or hulling

All sail is taken down.

The helm is lashed to leeward.

The boat takes up 'her own' position with respect to the seas.

Leaving the boat to fend for herself is not considered bad seamanship. Quite the contrary. It is a tactic to be employed when the wind is too strong to carry sail. Although the boat will probably lie nearly beam-on to the seas, the rolling motion will be more uncomfortable than dangerous.

The boat will move gradually at 1–2 knots to leeward and also make some headway due to the windage of the hull and rigging.

The *danger* in lying a-hull is that a freak wave will catch the boat, throw her on her side, damage the superstructure, or even capsize her.

Therefore, *if the waves reach dangerous heights the decision must be made to run with the storm.* **See: Running**

Lying a-hull/Riding to a sea anchor ■ 168

This provides maximum 'stopping' power.

The sea anchor may be streamed from either the bow or the stern.

A jib may be sheeted amidships or hanked on the backstay as a riding sail.

A sea anchor is a brutal brake against the seas which can produce a tremendous strain on the boat and, in effect, robs it of some buoyancy.

When a sea anchor is streamed from the stern, the boat is in danger of being pooped or pitch-poled.

When a sea anchor is streamed from the bow, the boat can easily be thrown backwards and the rudder damaged.

A sea anchor should only be used when the boat no longer has sea room, for example, on a lee shore.

For sea anchor techniques **See: Sea anchor**

Heavy weather

If you think heavy weather is on the horizon, you are already in it

A heavy weather check-list

Reef or change the sails.

Clear the deck and lash down all gear – do not trust elastic bands and snap fittings.

Check the lifelines and rig jackstays: **See: Safety harness**

Put on safety harnesses.

Record the last known position.

Record the barometer reading.

Prepare the sea anchor and warps.

Below: secure all lockers, especially those in the galley and containing tools and spares.

Empty the bilge.

Clear the cockpit drains.

Start the engine for a quick check, then close off the fuel line and the sea-cocks.

Close all other sea-cocks.

Close ventilators and exhausts.

Close the hawse pipe.

Secure the stormboards.

Put on all hatch covers.

Rig leeboards for the berths.

Start a pot of stew simmering on the stove.

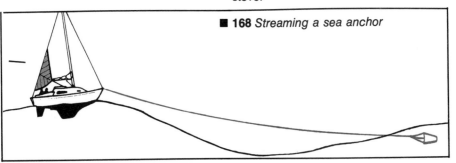

■ **168** *Streaming a sea anchor*

A decision must be made to:

1 – Continue on course under reduced sail. **See: Reefing and sail reduction, Stormsails**

2 – Head for port or shelter under reduced sail.

3 – Cope with the storm immediately by either:

1 – *Heaving-to*

Attempting to 'stop' or retard the movement of the boat

or

2 – *Running*

Allowing the boat to move with the direction of the storm, with or without a device, such as warps or a sea anchor, to slow her down.

If there is a possibility that a revolving storm – cyclone, hurricane or typhoon – is approaching **See: Law of storms**

Heaving-to

Advantages

The boat slows down and seems to 'stop', making only a little headway.

In general, little effort is required of the crew.

The boat assumes a 'natural' position which often increases comfort on board.

Disadvantages

The boat makes considerable leeway.

There is a risk of being thrown beam-on to the seas.

Deck-house, windows and hatches become vulnerable to wind and waves.

There is constant strain and chafe on sails and rigging.

Knock-downs and capsize may occur.

See: Heaving-to

Running

Advantages

Manoeuvrability is maintained and the boat 'steered' through the seas.

If the direction of the storm is favourable, progress on course can be made.

Strain and chafe on sails and rigging is minimized.

Disadvantages

A danger exists of being pooped, that is, having a following sea break over the stern.

Another danger is broaching – being thrown inadvertently beam-on to the seas.

In high waves, conceivably the boat could be pitch-poled – turned end over end.

Plenty of sea room is required.

Someone must always be at the helm.

The most vulnerable parts of the boat – the cockpit and aft bulkhead – are exposed to the seas.

See: Running

NOTE:

Beyond a certain point there can be no prescriptions. Variables such as sea state, wind force, hull design, strength of the crew, position, weather forecast, etc must be judged and weighed against the range of alternatives. Ultimately, each skipper must fall back on his own independent judgement.

If in doubt about whether to stay out to sea or run for harbour, *stay out to sea.*

Heliograph

A makeshift heliograph ■ 169

Materials

A glass mirror. Failing that any shiny piece of bright metal, such as the lid of a ration tin, beer can, or tobacco tin.

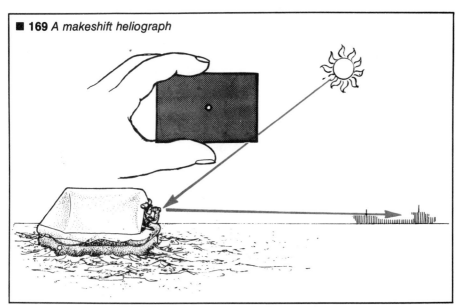

■ 169 *A makeshift heliograph*

Procedure

Punch a hole in the middle of the tin. With glass mirrors scrape away a bit of the silvering.

Hold the mirror or piece of tin a few inches from your face and sight the ship or aircraft through the hole.

Take your eye from the hole.

The sun's rays will pass through the hole on to your face or clothing.

Tilt the mirror or piece of tin until the reflection on your face or clothing disappears through the hole. At that point the sun will be reflected on to the target.

Don't worry about flashing the mirror or piece of tin as you will do this inadvertently.

NOTE:

Heliograph signals can often be seen 10 miles away. For the man in the liferaft or disabled boat, this means his signal might be seen by a rescue vessel or aircraft before he can see them. Thus, he should begin signalling as soon as he hears the sound of motors and can detect its direction.

Help!

See also: Distress signals

International Code of Signals

'V'

VICTOR

'I REQUIRE ASSISTANCE.'

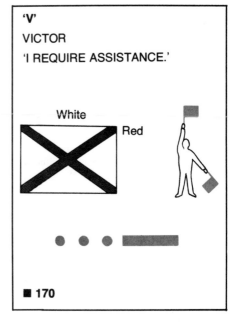

White

Red

■ 170

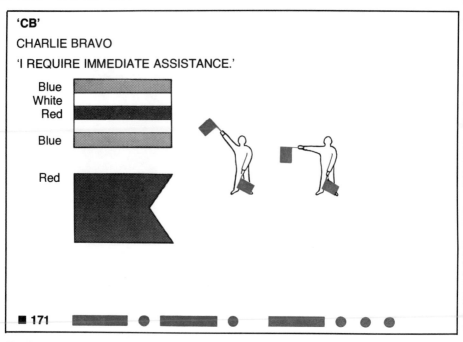

'CB'

CHARLIE BRAVO

'I REQUIRE IMMEDIATE ASSISTANCE.'

Blue
White
Red

Blue

Red

■ 171

Radio telephone signal

When requiring immediate assistance, but *not* in distress, the prefix 'PAN PAN PAN' should be used instead of 'MAYDAY!'

Holes

Immediate action

You must act immediately

By using damage control gear ■ **172.**

or

Stuffing the hole with cushions, sail bags, blankets, mattresses, or inflatable lifejackets (inflate the jackets when they are in place).

Clearing the area around the hole.

Backing the stuffing with wood – floorboards, tables, whatever is handy and malleable.

If the hole is on or near the waterline

Sail on the most favourable tack.

Heel the boat by shifting internal ballast, laying out the anchor chain, or running out a weighted boom.

Can the boat's pumping capacity cope with the inflow of water?

To estimate the boat's pumping capacity

Type of pump	Litres per minute
Manual	45–110
Electrical	45–110
Engine cooling	20–90
Engine driven	450–2000

To estimate the inflow of water

For a three-fingered sized hole	Litres per minute
Near the waterline	300
One metre below the waterline	500

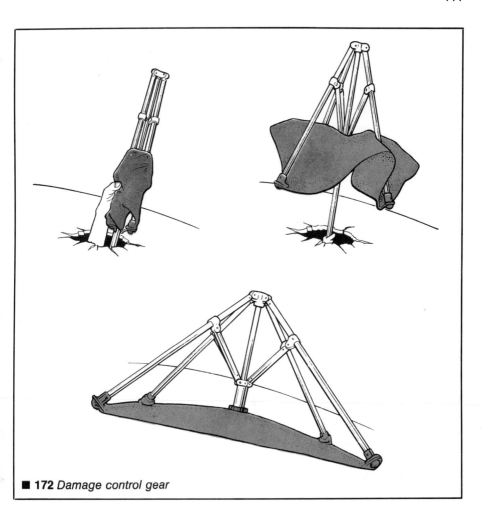

■ **172** *Damage control gear*

For a fist-sized hole

Near the waterline	600
One metre below the waterline	1200

Temporary repair

METHOD 1   Collision mat ■ 173

This can be manufactured quickly from a piece of canvas roughly one metre on a side, a weight or length of chain, and some line.

By adjusting the lines the mat can be positioned virtually anywhere on the hull. However, they must be kept taut, for if the mat is sucked into the hole it can easily be ripped.

NOTE:

The mat will make a tighter seal if it is backed with carpet or a layer of foam rubber. This can be cut from a mattress and stitched to the canvas. **See also: Leaks**

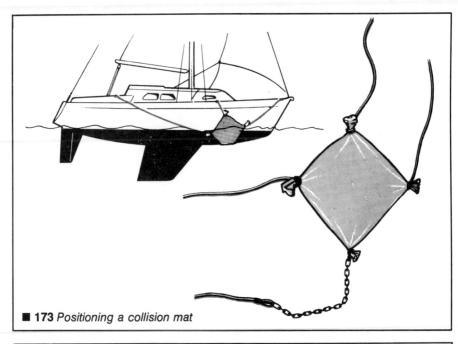

■ **173** *Positioning a collision mat*

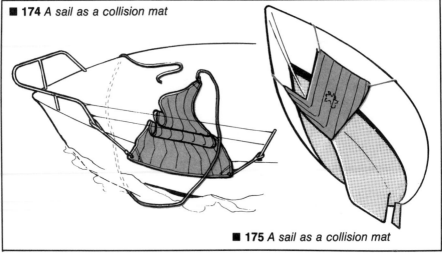

■ **174** *A sail as a collision mat*

■ **175** *A sail as a collision mat*

METHOD 2   A sail as collision mat
■ **174, 175**

A stormsail is preferable, and failing that a small jib.

Set the sail in place from the bow.

Make the tack and clew fast to a fitting fore and aft so that the foot is above the water-line ■ **174.**

Attach a rope to the head, and pass it under the bow.

Pull the head beneath the bow, then using the head and clew lines work the sail into position ■ **175.**

Keep the lines taut at all times.

METHOD 3   Cement

Mix one part cement with one part plaster.

Take an equal part of clay or dirt and add water until it becomes a runny mud.

Work the mud into the plaster-cement to form a putty.

Use immediately as the putty will begin to harden in a few minutes.

Apply the patch from outside the hull against a backing plate.

For other means of repair

See: Glass fibre repair, Aluminium repair, Wood repair, Steel hull repair, Ferrocement repair

Hull patches

See: Holes

Hurricanes

See: Law of storms

I

Ice

See: Water

Immersion foot

See also: Exposure

Symptoms

Legs or feet seem to 'fall asleep' to the point of insensitivity.

Swelling.

Toes become stiff.

Touch produces severe pain.

Treatment

Warm the feet or legs *slowly. Do not immerse in water!*

Wrap the feet or legs in rags or blankets which are at a moderate (warm) temperature.

Gradually warm the legs, moving from the body downwards, but do *not* rub or massage as this will damage the tissue.

Elevate the legs on soft cushions or pillows.

If infection develops, use antibiotics. **See: Antibiotics**

Do not walk until condition has improved.

Infection

Local infection

Symptoms

Part is red, hot, and tender.

Treatment

Localized collections of pus should be drained.

If necessary, take antibiotics. **See: Antibiotics**

Systemic infection, such as, pneumonia, septicaemia and strep. throat.

Symptoms

Fatigue

Loss of appetite.

General aches and pains.

Headache.

Temperature.

Increased pulse rate.

Perspiration.

NOTE:

Infections often arrive without warning and the symptoms appear rapidly.

Treatment

Rest.

Antibiotics. **See: Antibiotics**

Injections

For intramuscular injections ■ 176, 177, 178, 179

The target is the upper, outer quadrant of the buttocks.

Clean the area with alcohol ■ **176.**

Break the top of the ampule.

Insert the needle and fill the syringe by pulling out the plunger ■ **177.**

Then, hold it needle up and empty any remaining air by squeezing out a few drops of liquid ■ **178.**

With one hand squeeze a fold of flesh, and with the other hold the syringe like a pencil and jab it fast and forcefully on the target ■ **179.**

Release the fold and slowly squeeze out the contents of the syringe.

Quickly remove the syringe and cover the spot with a bit of cotton wool.

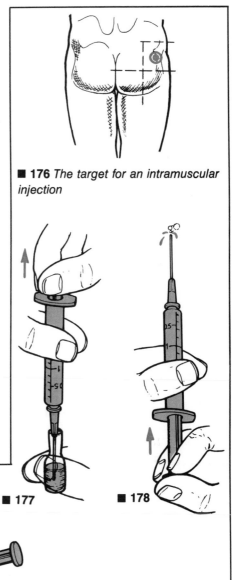

■ **176** *The target for an intramuscular injection*

Preparing the syringe

■ **177**

■ **178**

■ **179**

International code of signals

See: Anchoring, Danger, Disabled, Distress signals, Fire, Help!, Man overboard!, Medical assistance, Pilot, Stop, Towing

J

Jackstay

See: Safety harness

Jury-rigging

Temporary masts ■ 180, 181

Additional height can be had from the boom, spinnaker pole ■ 180A, an oar, or bits of the old mast lashed to the stump ■ 180B.

If the mast was stepped on the keel, the stump can be removed and the broken mast re-stepped.

If the mast is aluminium, often a section of the old mast can be lowered into the stump, wedged in with battens or floorboards, and lashed in place with wire or rope. If the break is high, trim down the stump before inserting the mast ■ 181.

Temporary shrouds and stays ■ 182, 183

Cable can be salvaged from the broken rigging, especially the upper shrouds which are longer, life-lines or the wire luff of sails.

Bend one end into a large strop, secured by Bulldog clamps. **See: Bulldog clamps**

Pass the strop over the cross-trees or hounds ■ 182, and fasten the other end to a deck fitting by a lashing, bottlescrew or Spanish windlass. **See: Lanyards, Spanish windlass**

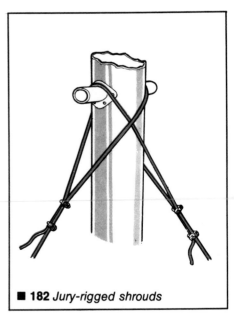

■ **182** *Jury-rigged shrouds*

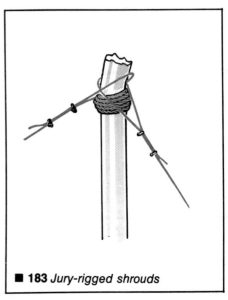

■ **183** *Jury-rigged shrouds*

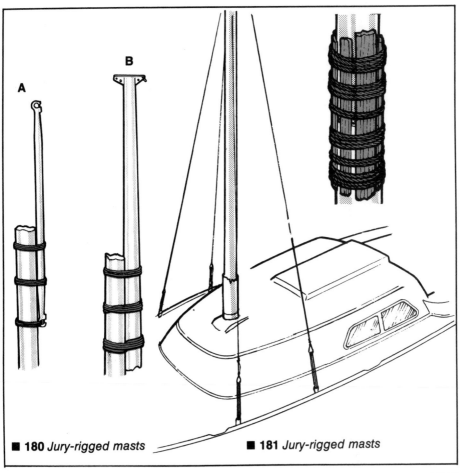

■ **180** *Jury-rigged masts*

■ **181** *Jury-rigged masts*

Temporary and movable cross-trees ■ 184

A spar or oar is loosely lashed at the foot of the mast and allowed to lean to windward.

A line from the masthead is tied to the end.

When in position – athwartships – the spar is guyed fore and aft.

When changing tacks, the entire system must be moved to the other side.

■ **184** *Temporary cross-trees*

118

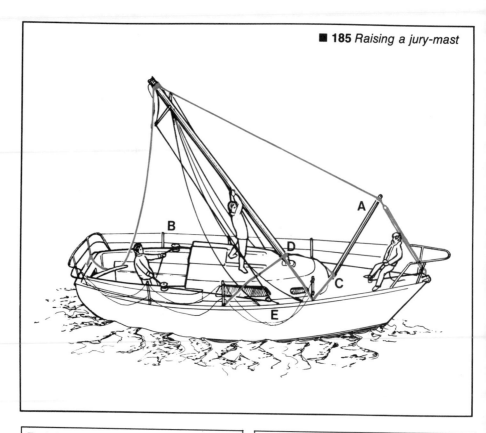

■ **185** *Raising a jury-mast*

Raising a jury-mast ■ 185

Bowse the foot of the broken mast to any available deck fitting, the mast stump or tabernacle ■ **185D**.

Loosely rig the backstay.

Attach lengths of line to the upper shrouds on both sides. Run the lines through blocks ■ **185E** at deck level and back to the cockpit winches ■ **185B**.

Rig a pair of sheer legs or a dead man ■ **185A** and brace it against the coachroof or a deck fitting ■ **185C**.

Attach the forestay to the upper end of the dead man ■ **185A** and a block and tackle from there to a fitting on the bow.

While hoisting the mast with the block and tackle from the bow, steady it with the cockpit winches.

Temporary halyards ■ 186

Shackles and blocks can be lashed to the top of the broken mast as high as possible. It may be necessary to notch the mast, or dent it with a hammer to prevent the lashing from sliding.

■ **186** *Temporary halyards*

Sail plans

In general – set as much sail as possible. Make the maximum use of smaller sails – jibs, storm-jibs and mizzens. If necessary a larger sail can be made smaller by simply knotting it.

See: Spanish reef ■ 187.

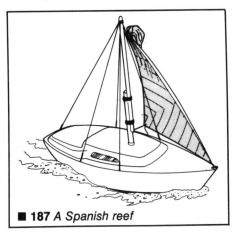

■ **187** *A Spanish reef*

Sloops and cutters

METHOD 1

Remove the boom, and turn the jib 90 degrees, or use a trysail as a loose-footed mainsail. A storm-jib or knotted jib becomes the foresail ■ **188.**

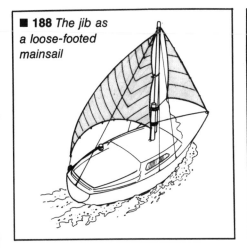

■ **188** *The jib as a loose-footed mainsail*

METHOD 2

Remove the boom and lash it to the mast as a topmast. A reefed mainsail is rigged loose-footed ■ **189.**

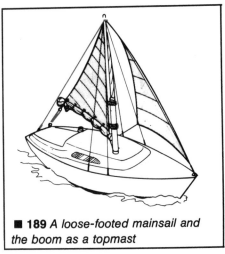

■ **189** *A loose-footed mainsail and the boom as a topmast*

METHOD 3

An oar or spinnaker pole is lashed at an angle to the mast stump, or if the mast is stepped in a tabernacle, the stump is canted aft. A single jib or genoa, upside down, is hoisted lateen style ■ **190.**

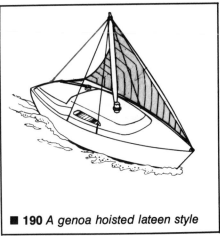

■ **190** *A genoa hoisted lateen style*

METHOD 4

A light, sprit boom is lashed to the old boom fitting. The spritsail is fabricated by removing the hanks from two jibs and joining them together with a tight lacing ■ **191.**

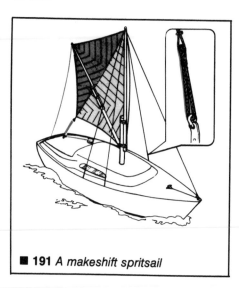

■ 191 *A makeshift spritsail*

Two-masted rigs

If the mizzen mast is still secure

METHOD 1

A mizzen staysail, jib or genoa, turned 90 degrees, is hoisted as a foresail ■ **192.**

■ 192 *The jib on its side*

METHOD 2

A temporary foremast is rigged. The storm-jib becomes the foresail, and the jib or mizzen staysail is hoisted as a mizzen staysail ■ **193.**

■ 193 *The jib as a mizzen staysail*

Jury rudders

A makeshift rudder using a sweep ■ 194, 195

Materials ■ 194

The shaft can be made from a boom, reinforced oars or the spinnaker pole.

The blade can be constructed from floorboards, or locker doors lashed or through-bolted to the shaft.

Procedure

The sweep is lashed to the stern, either to the pushpit, a stanchion, deck fitting, an 'X'-shaped crutch or, if necessary, a 'V' cut into the transom.

NOTE:

It is important to keep the turning point of the sweep as low as possible.

To prevent the oar from floating on the surface:

A small block and tackle is tied from the

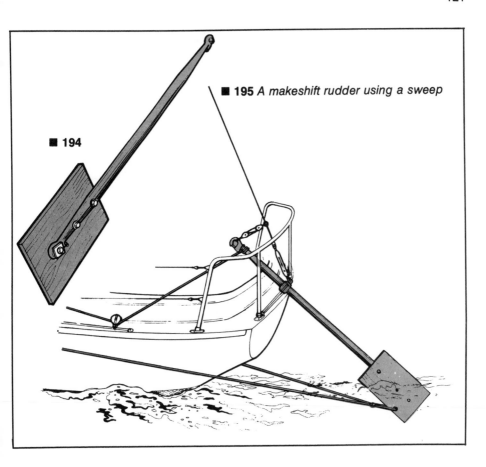

■ **194**

■ **195** *A makeshift rudder using a sweep*

handle to a bulldog clamp fixed to the backstay.

Weights, such as shackles or lengths of chain, are attached to the underside of the blade.

To obtain more leverage, and thus permit easier steering, a spar or oar can be lashed across the stern and blocks secured to the ends. The steering lines run from the blade, through the blocks to the cockpit winches ■ **196.**

To steer

Blocks and tackles can be tied to the inboard end of the sweep and secured

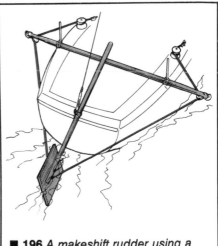

■ **196** *A makeshift rudder using a sweep and a spar for leverage*

port and starboard to the mizzen shrouds, deck fittings or stanchions ■ 197.

Lines from the blade can be run through blocks lashed on the stern and then to the cockpit winches.

If the boat has a pushpit, the spar should be lashed to the railing to give further support to the sweep which slides along it ■ 198.

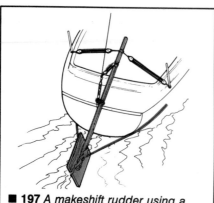

■ **197** *A makeshift rudder using a sweep with blocks and tackles for steering*

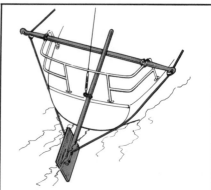

■ **198** *A makeshift rudder using a sweep with a spar for support*

A makeshift rudder, particularly for double-enders and counter sterns with nearly straight transoms ■ 199

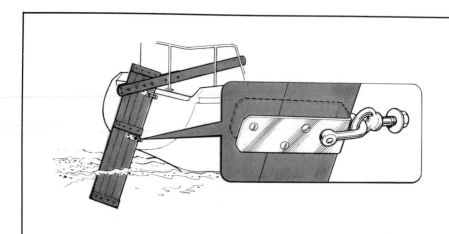

■ **199** *A makeshift rudder for double-enders and counter sterns*

Materials

The blade is fabricated from reinforced floorboards, bulkheads, locker doors or hatch covers.

The hinges are two eye-bolts and two shackles.

The metal reinforcing is cut from a pot.

The tiller is any spare piece of wood.

Procedure

Drill two holes for the eye-bolts in the transom, or for double-enders, left or right of the stern post.

Prepare the rudder itself and nail or screw on the metal reinforcing.

Connect the shackles to the eye-bolts.

Pass the bolt ends of the eye-bolts through the holes and securely bolt them in place.

A makeshift rudder, particularly for boats with pushpits ■ 200, 201, 202, 203, 204

Materials

The blade is fabricated from reinforced floorboards, bulkheads, locker doors or hatch covers ■ **200.**

The shaft is a spar, section of the pulpit or pushpit or a stanchion.

The tiller is cut from spare wood ■ **201.**

The sheave is cut from a length of pipe or strong plastic hose ■ **203.**

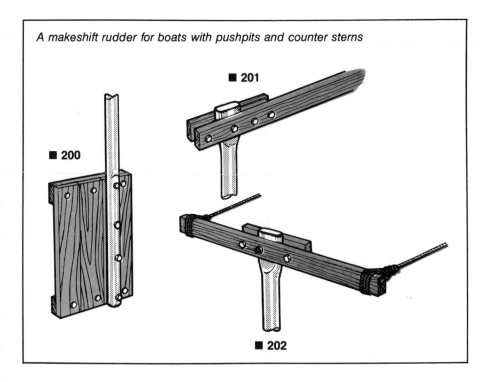

A makeshift rudder for boats with pushpits and counter sterns

■ 201

■ 200

■ 202

Procedure

The sheave is lashed in place ■ **203**.

The rudder and shaft are run through it.

Supporting lines from the blade are run forward and secured to stanchions or deck fittings ■ **204**.

A tiller ■ **201** or a yoke and lines ■ **202** is used for steering.

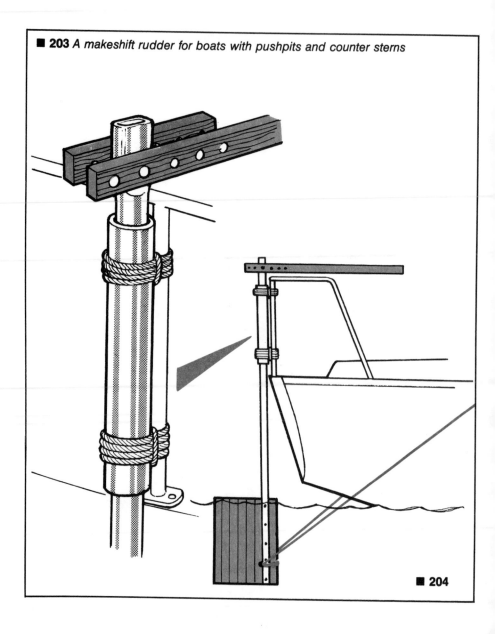

■ **203** *A makeshift rudder for boats with pushpits and counter sterns*

■ **204**

A makeshift rudder for boats without pushpits ■ 205

Procedure

The rudder can be lashed to a stern quarter.

A strong spar athwartships ■ **205A** is lashed to the cockpit winches, the coachroof, deck fittings or stanchions.

The sheave or rudder shaft is secured by a lashing to the spar ■ **205B.**

Supporting lines from the blade and the shaft are run fore and aft ■ **205C.**

NOTE:

It is preferable to lash the rudder on the leeward side so that the blade will be deeper in the water.

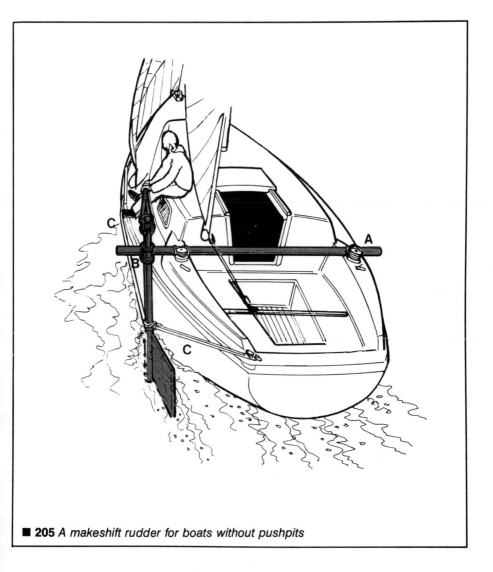

■ **205** *A makeshift rudder for boats without pushpits*

126

A makeshift rudder using a drogue ■ 206

Materials

The drogue can be a car tyre, sail bag full of rags, a jib or a small sea anchor.

A length of strong line.

A strong spar.

Procedure

The drogue is towed at least one full wavelength behind the boat.

The steering lines are tied to the warp with rolling hitches about 3–5 metres off the stern.

A strong spar is lashed athwartships on the stern, and blocks attached to either end.

The steering lines pass through the blocks and on to the cockpit winches.

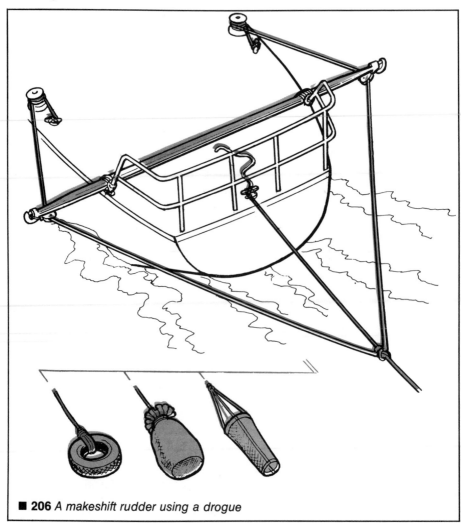

■ 206 *A makeshift rudder using a drogue*

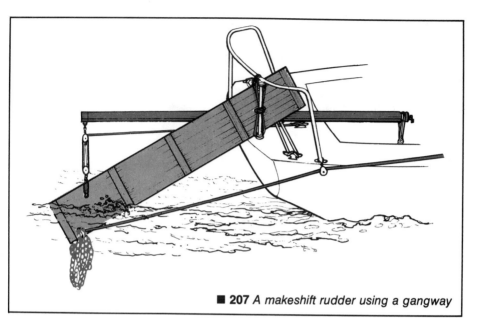

■ **207** *A makeshift rudder using a gangway*

A makeshift rudder using a gangway or a plank ■ 207

Procedure

Lash a spar, boom, or strong length of timber in place as a bumkin ■ **207A**.

NOTE:

In emergency conditions, the boom should be regarded as an available spar since the mainsail can always be rigged loose-footed. **See: Jury-rigging**

Tie a weight, such as a length of chain or a small anchor to the end of the gangway ■ **207B**.

Lash one end securely to the pushpit ■ **207C**.

By means of a block and tackle, or just a block, attach the other end of the gangway to the bumkin ■ **207D**. Run the line to the cockpit to control the angle of the blade ■ **207F**.

The steering lines are run from the end of the gangway forward to blocks and then on to the cockpit winches ■ **207E**.

A makeshift rudder using the jib boom or spinnaker pole ■ 208, 209

Procedure

Lash a spar, boom or a strong length of timber in place as a bumkin ■ **208A, 209A**.

A section of floorboard or plank is lashed or bolted to one end of the jib boom (or spinnaker pole) as a blade ■ **208B, 209B** and weighted with chain ■ **208C, 209C**.

Pass an eye-bolt through the rudder fitting and bolt it in place ■ **208D, 209D**.

The boom or pole fitting is clipped on to the eye-bolt.

The boom is supported by means of a line to a block attached to the end of the bumkin ■ **208E, 209E**.

Steering lines are run forward to blocks and then on to cockpit winches ■ **208F, 209F**.

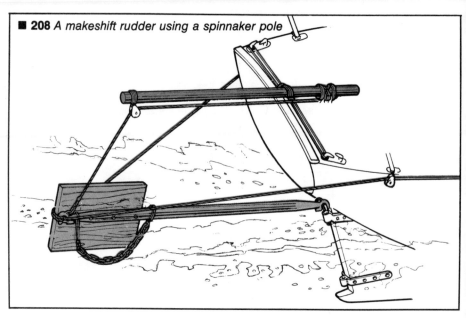

■ **208** *A makeshift rudder using a spinnaker pole*

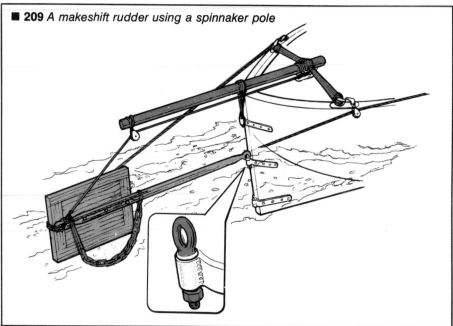

■ **209** *A makeshift rudder using a spinnaker pole*

Jury steering

See: Tiller

K

Kedging-off

See: Aground

Knots

Anchor bend ■ 210

To connect a warp with a ring or anchor.

Bowline ■ 211

Wherever a bight is needed.

See: Bowline – for a one-handed method.

■ 210

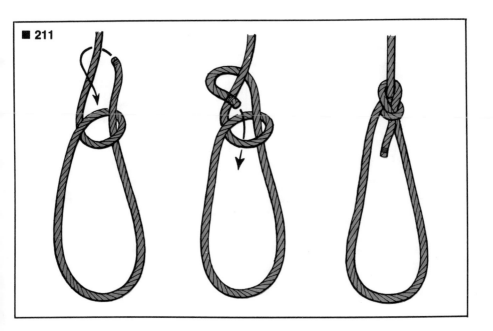

■ 211

Carrick bend ■ 212

To join heavy warps or lines of unequal size.

NOTE:

The ends can be tucked either over or under several times or bound to the line.

WARNING:

Do not use two bowlines to join lines together as this reduces their strength by about 50%.

Sheet bend ■ 213

To join a line to a bight or two lines of unequal size.
When joining two lines an extra turn should be taken making the knot into a double sheet bend.

Stopper knot or rolling hitch ■ 214

To make a line fast to a shroud, stay or spar which will not slip when pulled in one direction when pulled in the opposite direction from the knot.

■ 212

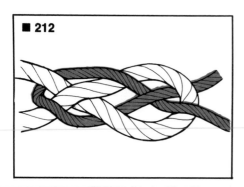

■ 213

■ 214

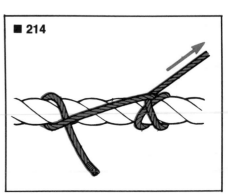

Tugboat hitch ■ 215

To attach a warp to a samson post or bollard.

■ 215

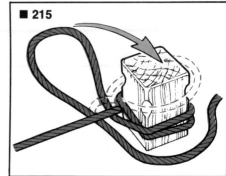

L

Landfall signs

Birds

The presence of birds cannot be taken as an indication that land is near. However, flight direction in the early evening is often a good indication of the bearing of land.

Breeze

Usually, a breeze comes from the land in the morning, and blows towards the land in the evening.

Clouds

Cumulus clouds

If they appear to be stationary in a clear sky, or when other clouds are moving rapidly, this should indicate land or an island.

A line of cumulus clouds

Often this will appear over and along a coastline.

A greenish-blue tint on the underside of the clouds

Occasionally, a flat cloud base may act as a mirror and reflect the green of a tropical island or a lagoon. This occurs most often in low latitudes.

A light tint on the underside of the clouds

This may be a reflection of an ice-field or snow covered land.

Surf

This can usually be heard long before it can be seen.

Colour of water

In general, the lighter the colour, the shallower the depth.

Smells

Those such as burning wood, swamps, and pollution often carry long distances, especially after a rain.

Winged insects

These do indicate the presence of land.

Landing signals

Landing signals for small boats made from shoreward or ashore

'THIS IS THE BEST PLACE TO LAND.'

By day

Vertical motion of a white flag.

Vertical motions of the arms.

A green star signal.

'K' — · — transmitted by either light or sound.

By night

Vertical motion of a white flare or light.

A green star signal.

'K' — · — transmitted by either light or sound.

'LANDING HERE IS HIGHLY DANGEROUS.'

By day

Horizontal motion of a white flag.

Horizontal motions of the arms.

A red star signal.

'S' · · · transmitted by either light or sound.

By night

Horizontal motion of a white flare or light.

A red star signal.

'S' · · · transmitted by either light or sound.

'LANDING HERE IS HIGHLY DANGEROUS. A MORE FAVOURABLE PLACE TO LAND IS IN THE DIRECTION INDICATED.'

By day

Horizontal motion of a white flag, followed by placing the flag in the ground and carrying another flag in the direction indicated.

By day or night

Horizontal motion of a white light or flare, followed by placing the light or flare on the ground and carrying another white light or flare in the direction to be indicated.

Firing a red star signal vertically, and a white star in the *direction of a better landing place.*

'S' · · · followed by 'R' · — · if the better landing is to the *Right of the approach line.*

'S' · · · followed by 'L' · — ·· if the better landing is to the *Left of the approach line.*

Lanyards

Lanyards can be used to replace broken bottlescrews, repair lifelines and set up damaged standing rigging. Six to eight turns of 1/8th inch Terylene line will equal the strength of small craft wire cable.

To form an eye on the end of a piece of broken wire cable **See: Bulldog clamps**

For rigging failures ■ 216, 217

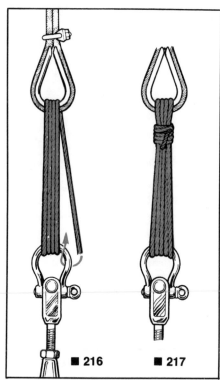

■ 216   ■ 217

For lifelines or lashings with a pull in only one direction ■ 218

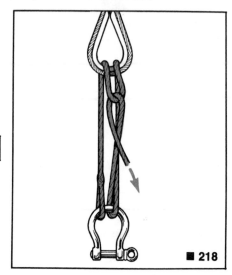

■ 218

Lashings

Lashing two spars together ■ 219, 220

Begin with a clove hitch.

Tuck the short end under the long one as you make the first turn.

Make at least two complete turns, pulling the line taut after each one.

End with a clove hitch or two half-hitches.

NOTE:

Whether lashing two spars together or at right angles to each other, the method is the same.

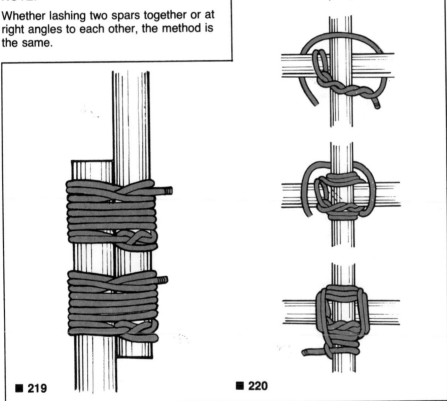

■ 219

■ 220

Latitude

See: Sextant – A Sun Sight without a sextant (p.206); **Sight Reduction Tables** – Latitude without Sight Reduction Tables – a 'Noon Sight' (p.213)

Law of storms

See also: Heavy weather

General indications of an approaching revolving storm

Cirrus and cirrostratus clouds.

Increasing humidity.

Sudden puffs of hot or cold wind.

A red, copper-coloured sky at sunrise and/or sunset.

An unsteady or falling barometer.

A heavy, unaccountable swell.

Unusual behaviour in sea birds.

One's position relative to the storm

In the northern hemisphere

When an observer faces the wind – the storm's centre is approximately 110 degrees to his right.

Then:

If the wind veers to the right, he is in the right-hand semi-circle, that is, the centre of the storm will pass to his right.

If the wind moves to the left and backs, he is in the left-hand semi-circle, that is, the centre of the storm will pass to his left.

If the wind is constant in direction, but increasing in force, he is directly in the path of the storm *or* directly behind it.

If the barometer falls – he is in front of the storm centre.

If the barometer rises, he is behind the storm centre.

In the northern hemisphere, the most dangerous semi-circle is to the right of the path of the storm.

NOTE:

In the southern hemisphere all directions are the reverse.

If in the direct path of the storm

Run with the wind on the starboard quarter. **See: Running**

If in the right-hand semi-circle

Heave-to on the starboard tack. **See: Heaving-to**

If in the left-hand semi-circle

Run with the wind on the starboard quarter. **See: Running**

Leaks

A checklist for leaks

Sea-cocks: galley, toilet, engine intake and exhaust, bilge pumps

Through hull fittings

Stuffing box

Water tank

The hull: along the stem, garboards, transom, hull-deck connections, keel

Quick repair

Caulk with: caulking cotton, greased rags, underwater epoxy, bandages, foam rubber, plugs and towels.

Repairs

See: Glass fibre repair, Wood repair, Aluminium repair, Steel hull repair, Ferrocement repair

For emergency repair of holes See: Holes

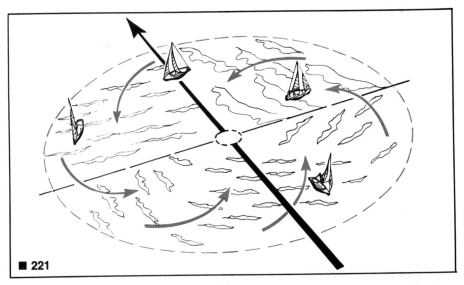

■ 221

Lee shore

Getting underway from a lee shore under sail ■ 222

With a dinghy, lay out a second anchor off the bow and tie the warp to the stern ■ 222A. See: Anchoring

Hoist the sails but do NOT sheet them in.

Haul in the stern warp until the boat is beam on to the wind ■ 222B.

Raise the bow anchor.

Let go and buoy the stern warp ■ 222C.

Sheet in the sails and sail away close-hauled ■ 222D.

For anchoring on a lee shore See: Anchoring

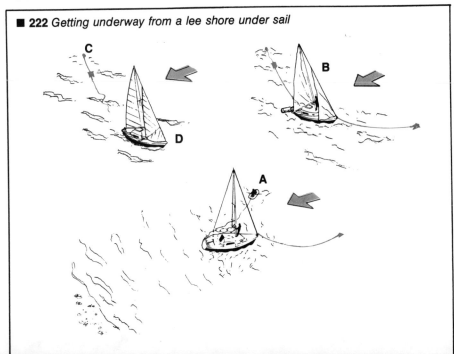

■ 222 Getting underway from a lee shore under sail

Liferaft

Launching ■ 223

Tie the operating line to a secure point, for example, a stanchion or the lifeline.

Throw the entire container or valise overboard.

Pull the operating line to inflate the raft.

Full inflation should occur within a minute.

Board the raft, *then* cut the painter.

If the raft cannot be brought alongside, jump directly on to the raft. **See: Abandon ship!**

NOTE:

Do *not* remove wet clothing, as even that provides some insulation and shelter from the elements.

■ **223** *Launching a liferaft*

Getting the injured aboard ■ 224, 225

Once alongside the raft, turn the injured man so that his back faces the raft's door.

Grasp him under the armpits.

Push him *down* into the water ■ **224.**

The buoyancy of his body and the lifejacket he should be wearing will thrust him upwards so he can easily be pulled on board ■ **225.**

■ **224** *Getting the injured aboard*

■ **225** *Getting the injured aboard*

NOTE:

To reach someone injured, motionless, or who can't swim, don't leave the liferaft. Instead, pull in the drogue, roll it into a ball, throw it in the direction of the survivor and pull the liferaft to him.

Heavy weather

A sea anchor or drogue should be streamed to hold the raft up to the wind and waves. Often its effectiveness can be improved by adding a riding weight.

Some castaways report that in high seas, *deflating* the raft slightly can be advantageous. It allows the raft to shape itself to the waves, rather than present a rigid and vulnerable profile. **See: Sea anchor**

Capsize ■ 226

A cloth loop and the gas cylinder are usually found on the bottom of most rafts. Using these a swimmer can climb on to the over-turned raft. He should attempt to point the raft into the wind, wait for the right wave, then lean backwards and pull the raft upright.

If there is no handhold on the bottom of the raft, the painter can be carried across the underside and used as a lever.

■ **226** *Righting an over-turned liferaft*

Repairs

Clamp repair procedure ■ 227, 228, 229

Dip plug in water to make the insertion easier.

Push the bottom plate through the hole in the fabric. If the hole is too small, enlarge it carefully so the plate can just be forced in ■ 227.

Pull the bottom plate back against the inner fabric surface and screw down the top plate against the outer fabric surface ■ 228.

Hold the loose edges in place while adjusting the clamp to cover the hole completely.

Screw down the wing nut firmly ■ 229.

Patches

Dry and clean the surface where the patch is to be applied.

Select a patch large enough to have a safety margin of at least one inch all round the hole.

Roughen the surface of the area to be patched.

Apply cement to both the patch and the area round the hole. Allow to dry, then apply a second coat and a third.

When the cement becomes tacky, press the patch on evenly and securely.

If possible do not inflate the raft hard until the patch has had 24 hours to dry.

Plugs

These are generally used for larger holes.

The fabric is drawn around the plug and securely bound with cord to make an airtight seal.

NOTE:

Nearly all liferafts are designed to withstand a *minimum* of 30 days at sea in the worst of conditions. A great deal of the water comes from the flexing of the fabric, for this reason the chambers should be kept as rigid as possible.

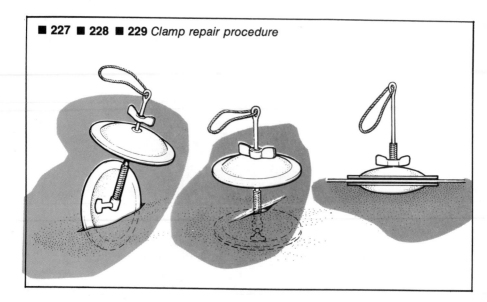

■ 227 ■ 228 ■ 229 *Clamp repair procedure*

Strategy

Wait for help to arrive?

or

Begin sailing towards the nearest shore?

Circumstances should dictate this decision. Where they don't, the gambler's choice is to make sail.

Besides the psychological boost of 'doing something' instead of just 'waiting around', often the closer one is to land the more traffic there is at sea.

Judging from the experience of recent castaways, such as the Robertsons and the Baileys, the sooner a castaway accepts the fact that he is on his own, the better. Even with the best emergency radio gear, flares, and radar reflectors, equipment can malfunction, freighters be piloted by sleepy watches and radar scanners rotate only for regulations. Numerous ships passed close to the Robertsons and the Baileys before they were finally rescued. Viewing the liferaft as a sailing boat may well be the only means to survival.

If a distress signal has been broadcast, a reasonable length of time to wait for help is five days. After that time the statistical chances of rescue fall off dramatically.

If land is in sight

There is usually an on-shore wind in the mornings, and often in the afternoons as well. In those conditions the sea anchor should be streamed only at night.

If land is not in sight

See: Landfall signs

Progress can *only* be made to leeward.

When the wind is unfavourable, a sea anchor should be streamed to 'park' the raft.

Progress can be made, depending on wind conditions, up to as much as 40 miles a day. This can be achieved by either hoisting a make-shift sail or holding the raft's entry port into the wind by means of a half-tripped sea anchor ■ **230.**

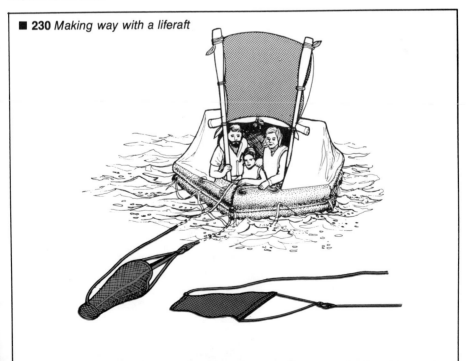

■ **230** *Making way with a liferaft*

Food from the sea

Fish

Do *not* eat fish that have spines or bristles instead of scales. **See: Fishing**

Do *not* eat fish which puff themselves up into a ball.

Do *not* eat fish which are pallid at the gills.

Do *not* eat fish which have been left in the sun for more than two hours.

Do *not* eat shark livers.

Do eat the heart, liver and brains of fish as often they are more nourishing than the flesh.

Eat fish only if fresh water is available. Fish are salty and the digestive process draws more on the body's supply of water than other types of food.

For fishing methods and preserving **See: Fishing**

Barnacles and shellfish

Barnacles will often grow on the under side of the raft or on trailing lines. All are edible, *except* if they have lived on surfaces coated with anti-fouling.

Crabmeat is edible except for the loose, finger-like spongy material around the edge of a de-shelled crab, and the stomach, which is just below the head.

Birds ■ 231, 232, 233, 234, 235, 236

All sea birds are edible.

They can be caught by fish hooks, baited with small pieces of wood or metal, or by hand. When trying to seize them by hand, wait until the bird has settled and folded its wings before attempting to grab it.

Birds should be skinned rather than plucked.

Provided fresh water which aids digestion has been drunk that day, drink the bird's blood.

Eat the entrails first, as the meat may be dried and preserved.

Turtles

They are best caught by their flippers, hauled into the raft and killed while on their back. Thrust a knife into the neck in order to cut the veins and arteries on both sides.

Drink the blood immediately before it coagulates. The meat can be cut in strips, eaten straight away or dried.

Plankton and seaweed

These can be caught by trailing a fine weave net. However, they should be washed in *fresh* water before eating, as some varieties are *toxic*. Eat them only as a last resort.

Water

Drink as much as you can before boarding the liferaft.

In the raft, do not drink for the first 24 hours.

Do *not* drink sea-water. Although the body can tolerate a small amount, its salt content is three times more than the body can cope with. Also, do not mix salt water with fresh water.

NOTE:

In moderate conditions a person can survive five or six days without water and not suffer any permanent body damage.

Do not eat unless you have some water to drink. The digestive process consumes body fluid.

If possible, drink your water ration in small quantities at several times during the day.

Collect any morning dew from the cold surfaces of the raft.

Since most body water is lost through perspiration, keeping the body cool by clothing soaked in sea water is a vital means of conservation.

See: Rainwater, Solar still, Water

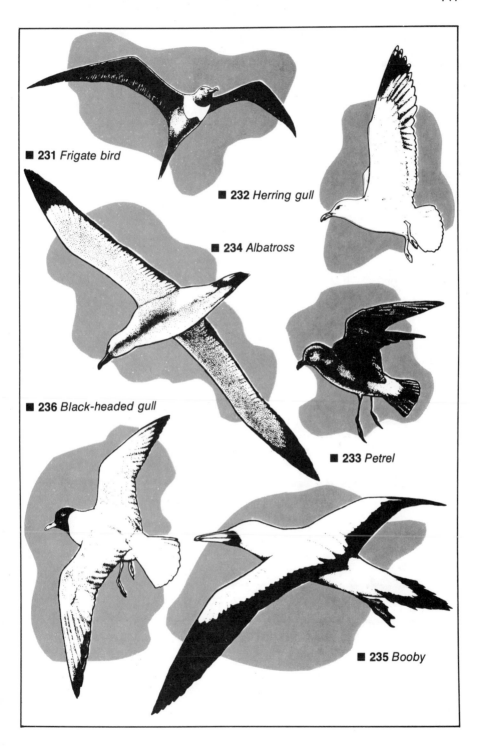

■ **231** *Frigate bird*

■ **232** *Herring gull*

■ **234** *Albatross*

■ **236** *Black-headed gull*

■ **233** *Petrel*

■ **235** *Booby*

■ 237 *Landing a liferaft in a heavy swell*

Landing ■ 237

If possible, do not land with on-shore wind *and* waves.

Stream a sea anchor, and prepare an emergency one.

Cut away the canopy so that no one will be trapped inside should the raft pitch-pole.

Persons should be fully clothed, wearing life-jackets, oilskins and whatever else is available for protection against rocks or coral.

When near the surf, all occupants should move towards the seaward side to maintain the raft's stability.

If the surf is extremely heavy, the raft may need to be flooded in order for it to remain stable.

Should the raft capsize, stay with the raft as long as possible.

WARNING:

Always attempt to land on the lee side of coral islands or atolls.

Attempt to land only at high tide when the waves may pass over the reef without breaking.

Do not attempt a landing at night.

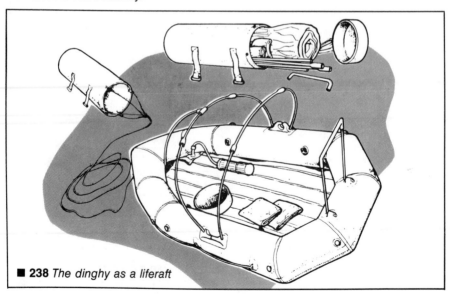

■ 238 *The dinghy as a liferaft*

The dinghy as a liferaft ■ 238, 239, 240

■ **239** *The dinghy as a liferaft*

Materials

A bucket, which will serve as a storage container, bailer and drogue.

A canopy against exposure: preferably Day-Glo in colour, it should have a large entrance opening at one end and a smaller port at the other to control the drogue. The canopy can be drawn over the dinghy like a sausage skin and tied in place.

Wooden or aluminium struts to hold the canopy erect.

Shockcords to lash emergency flotation in place.

Flotation: inner tubes, expanded polystyrene packing, cushions, empty bottles, spare life-jackets, fenders. A normal-sized tubular fender will have about 25–30kg. of positive buoyancy, and the yacht's supply, if securely lashed in place, can make a small dinghy unsinkable.

NOTE:

If the dinghy is an inflatable it should be let on deck half-inflated during a passage.

■ **240** *The dinghy as a liferaft*

Lightning storms

In severe electrical storms

The crew should go below.

The helmsman should avoid any contact with a metal part of the boat.

Lightning, like most natural phenomena, is not totally predictable. But as a general rule: it will strike the top of the mast. From there it will take the shortest path, via metal, to the water. Should there be a gap in this circuit the lightning bolt will burn its way through. Metal objects within two metres from this path are susceptible to side flashes.

Steel hulls

The rigging and hull act as a conductor, provided the shrouds are well connected (in an electrical sense) to the hull.

Wood and GRP hulls

The most likely place to find a break in the circuit is between the chain plates of the upper shrouds and the water.

Temporary protection

A piece of thick cable, preferably copper, can be bonded to the base of the upper shrouds and the other end dropped in the water. If possible, a piece of screen or thin metal plate should be attached to the end to help diffuse the electricity.

or

A length of chain can be well bonded to the shrouds and dropped in the water.

Lightning protection

It is quite *unlikely* that a yacht will be struck by lightning, and if so, that she will be damaged.

None the less, a lightning rod (conductor), at least six inches long, should be mounted on top of the mast, particularly if the mast is wooden. All other metallic instruments, anemometers, radio aerials, etc., should be grounded (earthed) to the rod to prevent side flashes.

This rod, if properly grounded (earthed), will provide the boat with a 'protective cone', the sides of which will be at an angle of about 60 degrees from the mast.

At the other end, on non-metallic boats, a copper strip should be connected between the chain plates on both sides and the keel bolts. If there is no external ballast, a small copper plate should be fixed to the outside of the hull and the cable connected to it. One shouldn't worry about grounding the forestay or the backstay as the circuit via the shrouds will nearly always be shorter.

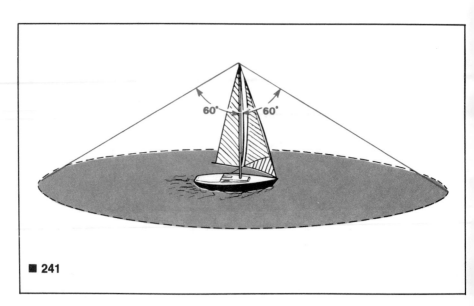

■ 241

Lights

Power vessels

Underway: masthead light forward, sidelights and a stern light.

If over 50 metres: a second masthead light abaft and higher than the forward one ■ 242.

A vessel constrained by her draft

For instance a supertanker: three red lights in addition to her normal steaming lights ■ 243.

■ **242** A power vessel underway

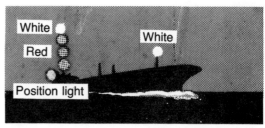

■ **243** A vessel restricted in her ability to manoeuvre

Fishing vessels (over 50 metres)

Trawling: white all-round light aft and green over white lights forward ■ 244.

Trawling in pairs: searchlight forward and in the direction of the other pair ■ 245.

■ **244** A fishing vessel engaged in trawling

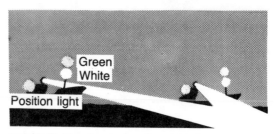

■ **245** Fishing boats trawling in pairs

Fishing vessels over 20 metres but not engaged in trawling: red over white lights ■ 246.

■ **246** A fishing boat engaged in fishing

Hovercraft

Flashing yellow light (120 flashes per minute) ■ **247.**

■ **247** *Hovercraft*

Pilot ship on duty

At anchor white over red near the masthead ■ **248.**

■ **248** *A pilot ship at anchor*

Vessel aground

Two red lights ■ **249.**

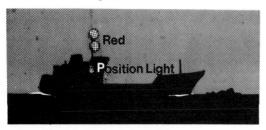

■ **249** *A vessel aground*

For light patterns of ships at anchor, See: Anchoring

For light patterns of ships under tow, See: Towing

Lighthouse characteristics

Fixed (F.): a continuous steady light.

Flashing (Fl.): single flash at regular intervals. Duration of light always less than the period of darkness.

Group Flashing (Gp.Fl.): two or more brilliant flashes in succession at regular intervals.

Isophase (Iso.): duration of light and darkness are equal.

Occulting (Occ.): steady light with total eclipse at regular intervals. Duration of darkness less than that of light.

Quick Flashing (Qk.Fl.): continuous flash at rate of 50 or 60 per minute.

Group Occulting (Gp.Occ.): two or more eclipses in a group at regular intervals.

Alternating (Alt.): a light which alters in colour in successive flashes or eclipses.

Lloyd's

Reporting through Lloyd's

At sea any ship may be asked to report a yacht to Lloyd's of London. The international code signal is 'ZD2'.

The ship will send a telegramme to Lloyd's giving the name of the yacht, its position, and any other message. The cost of the service is paid by the owner of the yacht, hence arrangements with Lloyd's should be made before a passage.

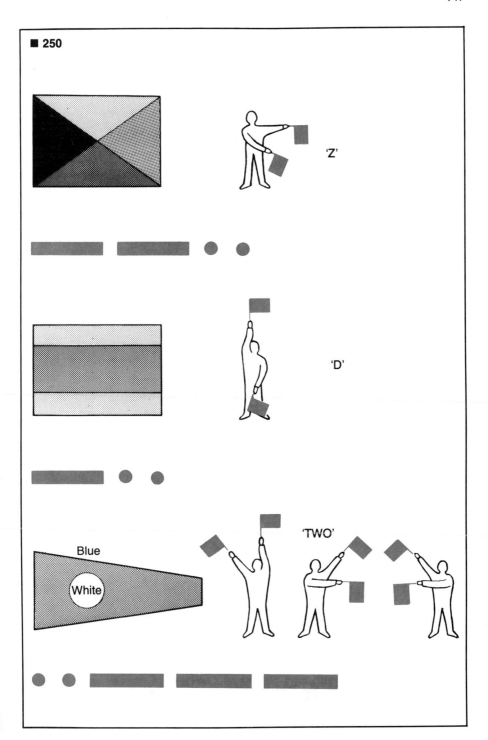

■ 250

'Z'

'D'

Blue

White

'TWO'

148

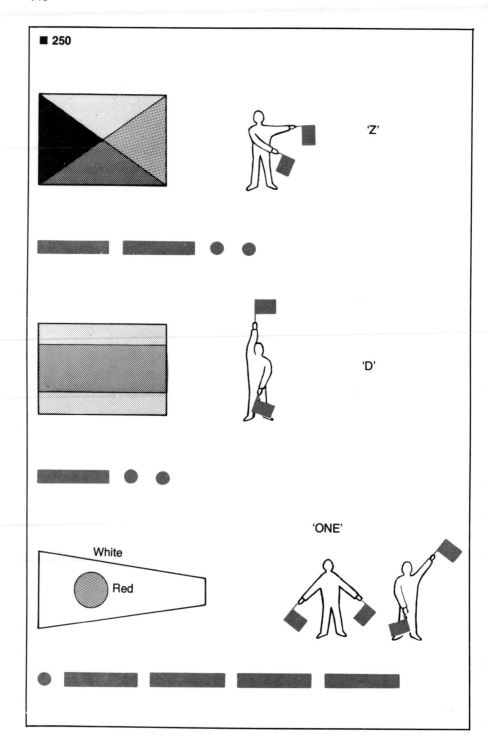

Reporting through the United States' Coast Guard

To report to the U.S. Coast Guard in New York the signal is 'ZD1'.

Log

An emergency log ■ 251

Materials

A kitchen or fuel-oil funnel.

Elastic bands.

50 metres of line.

A watch.

Procedure

One end of the line is tied to the small end of the funnel.

Elastic bands form a harness to the funnel's large end and are lashed to the line.

Two knots are tied exactly 30.5 metres apart.

The funnel is thrown overboard and the line runs out freely.

When the first knot passes through your hand, timing begins, and ends when the second knot appears.

Seconds	Knots
120 =	$\frac{1}{2}$
60 =	1
30 =	2
20 =	3
15 =	4
12 =	5
10 =	6

To pull in the log, a quick tug on the line will stretch the elastic bands and pitch-pole the funnel.

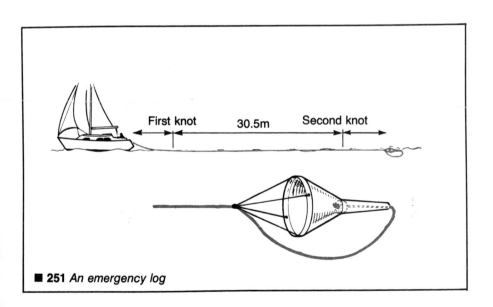

■ 251 *An emergency log*

Speed from distance

If distance travelled – from the log – is
timed, the boat's speed can easily be
calculated.

Time	Speed												
	2	3	4	5	6	7	8	9	10	11	12	13	14
0 h 05	0.2	0.2	0.3	0.4	0.5	0.6	0.7	0.7	0.8	0.9	1.0	1.1	1.2
0 h 10	0.3	0.5	0.7	0.8	1.0	1.2	1.3	1.5	1.7	1.8	2.0	2.2	2.3
0 h 15	0.5	0.7	1.0	1.2	1.5	1.7	2.0	2.2	2.5	2.7	3.0	3.2	3.5
0 h 20	0.7	1.0	1.3	1.7	2.0	2.3	2.7	3.0	3.3	3.7	4.0	4.3	4.7
0 h 25	0.8	1.2	1.7	2.1	2.5	2.9	3.3	3.7	4.2	4.6	5.0	5.4	5.8
0 h 30	1.0	1.5	2.0	2.5	3.0	3.5	4.0	4.5	5.0	5.5	6.0	6.5	7.0
0 h 45	1.5	2.2	3.0	3.7	4.5	5.2	6.0	6.7	7.5	8.2	9.0	9.7	10.5

Distance

Longitude

See: Sextant – Longitude without a sextant (p.206), A Sun Sight
without a sextant (p.206), **Sight reduction tables** – Finding
Longitude without Sight Reduction Tables (p.212)

Lost!

One is never lost in the full sense of the
word, that is, cast on an unknown ocean
without bearings or boundaries.

Some facts are always known, or at least
can be approximated.

1 – A previous position, if only your
starting point.

2 – The time since you left that point,
even if it is no more than a reasonable
guess.

3 – An estimation of maximum speed. If
not your actual speed, at least the
maximum possible speed, allowing for
drift, tide and current.

Speed × *Time* = *The Maximum
Distance* travelled since your last known
position. If that distance becomes the
radius of a circle, your position *must* be
somewhere within it ■ 252.

4 – An estimation of minimum speed,
allowing for drift, tide and current. By
multiplying this speed by Time, your
minimum distance from your last
known position is found. When this is
plotted along the radius, the inner
portion of the circle can be eliminated
■ 253.

Speed × Time = Maximum Distance Travelled   Last known position

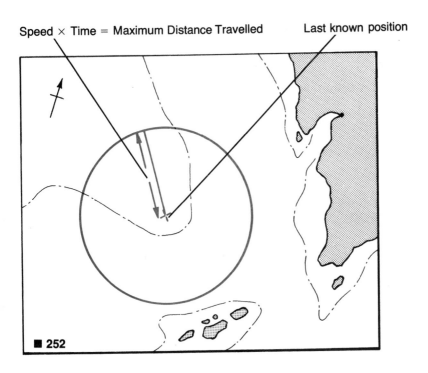

■ 252

Area of your possible position   Maximum Distance   Minimum Distance

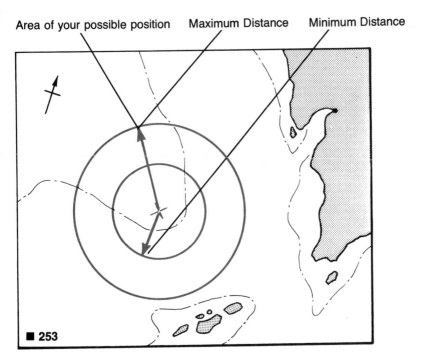

■ 253

5 – If the boat's compass functions, your course, or, at the very least, a guess whose error would be no more than plus or minus 45 degrees.

Plotting that course as a radius eliminates three quadrants of the circle. Your position must be somewhere within the remaining section ■ 254.

Land is *not* in sight

To estimate more closely your position, additional navigational information is necessary:

A reading from an echo sounder. **See: Echo sounder**

An RDF bearing. **See: Radio direction finder**

An astro-navigational sight. **See: Longitude, Latitude, Stars**

See: Landfall signs

Land is in sight

The distance-off can be estimated. **See: Distance at sea, Distance-off**

To establish an exact 'fix' some additional navigational information is necessary:

A bearing to an identifiable point ashore.

A reading from the echo sounder. **See: Echo sounder**

An RDF bearing. **See: Radio direction finder**

An astro-navigational sight. **See: Longitude, Latitude, Stars**

Area of your possible position   Your estimated course

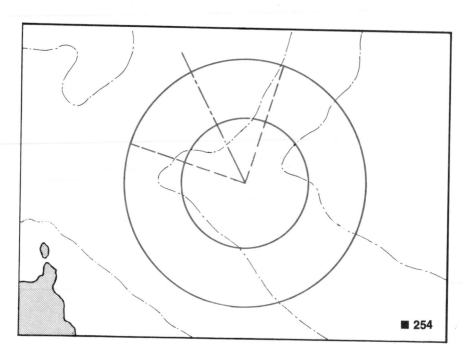

■ 254

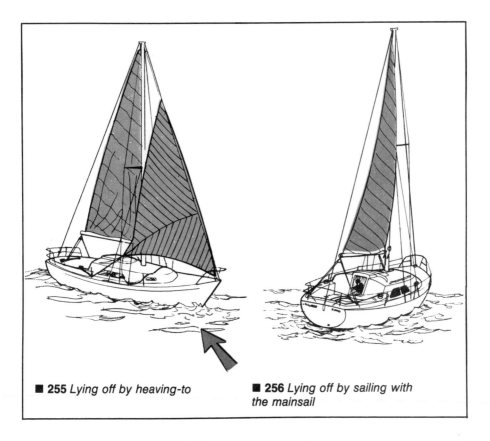

■ **255** *Lying off by heaving-to*

■ **256** *Lying off by sailing with the mainsail*

Lying off

When waiting for dawn, port signals, a tide change, or a pilot it may be necessary to 'stop' the boat and maintain position.

METHOD 1   Heaving-to ■ 255

In general, back a jib or staysail, and sheet in the mainsail ■ . **The tiller is lashed to leeward.**

See: Heaving-to

METHOD 2   Anchoring

See: Anchoring

METHOD 3   A sea anchor

Stream a sea anchor from either the bow or the stern. **See: Sea anchor**

METHOD 4   Drifting

The boat can be left to drift with the helm lashed a-lee.

METHOD 5   Sailing with the mainsail ■ 256

The mainsail is sheeted in hard, and the helm lashed a-lee.

NOTE:

A boat hove-to or lying-to is still by law underway even if she is making no way.

M

Man overboard!

International Code of Signals

'O'

OSCAR

'MAN OVERBOARD!'

Red

Yellow

■ 257

Emergency action

Do *not* turn immediately.

Throw *some* buoyancy aids over the side.

Also throw any brightly coloured objects – such as cockpit cushions, bottles, oilskins, clothing – in the water which will float and mark the spot.

At least one person should keep his eyes *only* on the man in the water.

Start the engine.

Then begin to manoeuvre.

The basic 'Man overboard!' manoeuvre ■ 258

Immediately, turn upwind ■ 258A.

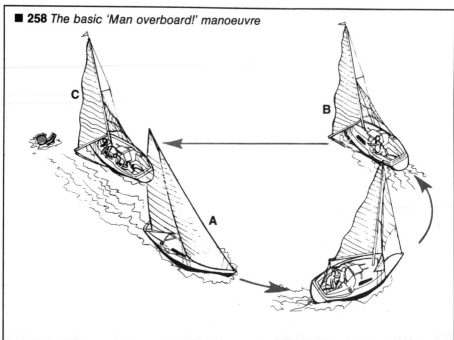

■ 258 *The basic 'Man overboard!' manoeuvre*

C

B

A

Sail on a circular course which will put you to windward of the man in the water ■ **258B.**

Come about, but leave the jib backed.

When directly to windward of the man in the water, let fly the mainsheet and put the helm to leeward ■ **258C.**

In this 'heave-to' position the boat will drift broadside towards the man in the water.

Drift can be corrected by hauling and slackening the mainsheet or using the rudder.

NOTE:

The man in the water can use the slackened main sheet to help him climb on board.

The man overboard is in sight

Pick up from a reach ■ **259, 260.**

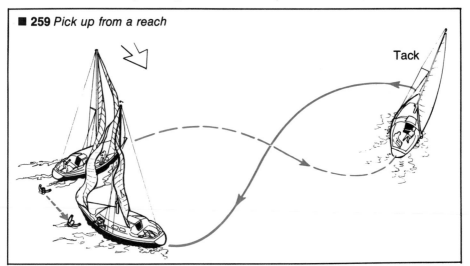

■ **259** *Pick up from a reach*

Tack

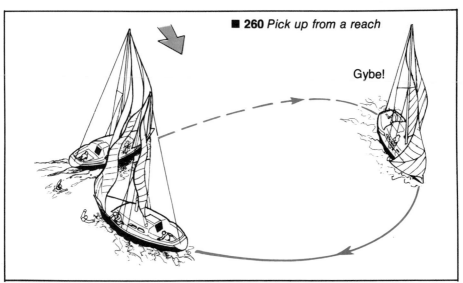

■ **260** *Pick up from a reach*

Gybe!

Pick up from a windward course ■ 261

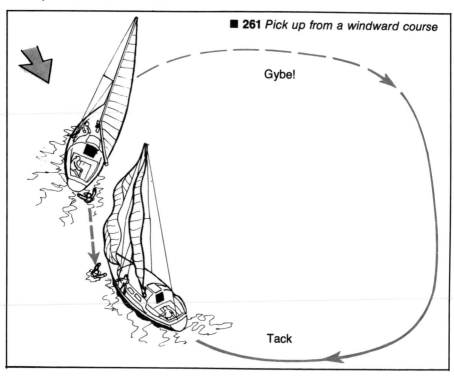

■ **261** *Pick up from a windward course*

Gybe!

Tack

Pick up from a downwind course ■ 262

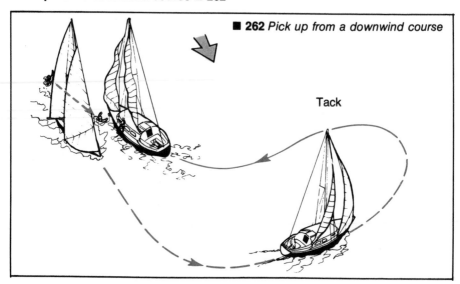

■ **262** *Pick up from a downwind course*

Tack

The man overboard is not in sight ■ 263, 264, 265

Fix your position.

Note time and course.

If little wind, no current, and good visibility

Sail, or preferably motor, on a reciprocal course.

If conditions are unfavourable

Begin a planned search pattern at once.

As a general rule, one should sail back well *past* the estimated point at which the man went overboard.

Then the boat should sail back and forth across his estimated course on parallel tracks.

These tracks should be timed, either by a verbal count or a watch.

The first track should be only half that of all of the remaining tracks. The distance between tracks must be carefully calculated to be clearly within the limits of visibility.

Searching from a windward course ■ 263

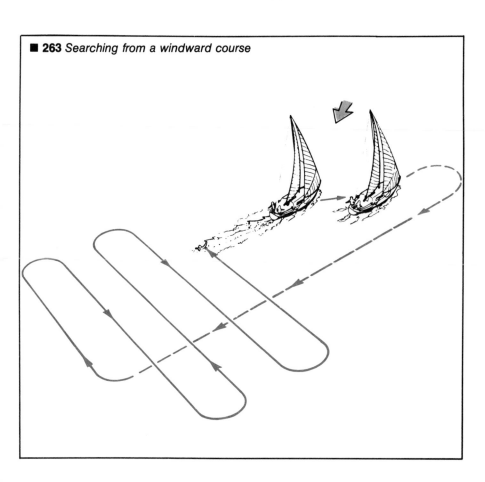

■ **263** *Searching from a windward course*

Searching from a reach ■ 264

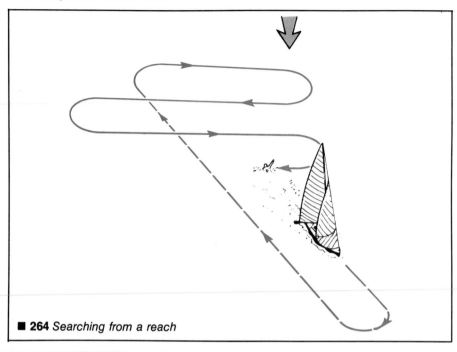

■ **264** *Searching from a reach*

Searching from a downwind course ■ 265

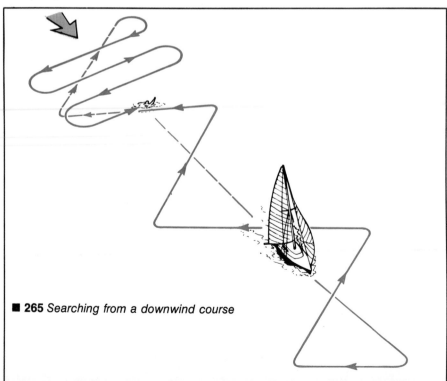

■ **265** *Searching from a downwind course*

NOTE:

Floating safety gear will probably drift faster to leeward than the man in the water. Hence, if liferings, etc., are found first, the survivor is more than likely somewhere to windward.

For the man in the water

Remove any weights from pockets.

Remain fully clothed. As a general rule, clothing will keep the skin temperature 4–5 degrees above the water temperature.

Remove any brightly coloured garments which can be used for signalling.

Do *not* swim after the boat. Conserve energy, especially if the water is cold. Float on your back with your head into the waves.

Don't shout, as this will also tire you out.

For a temporary set of water wings, remove your trousers, knot the legs, then whip them over your head and into the water. Lie in the crotch.

If you receive a line, tie a one-handed bowline. **See: Bowline**

NOTE:

Don't panic. Remember that when in the water one's horizon is very near – in a calm sea, perhaps no more than a mile. The boat may therefore seem to sail out of sight before turning.

Bringing the man on board
■ **266, 267, 268**

On small boats pick up the survivor on the *windward* side or the *stern*.

On larger boats, on the *lee* side.

Stop the engine.

Slacken the lifelines.

Don't lower a rope. Lower a bight.

With a bowline on the end.

With both ends securely cleated on deck.

With one end wound on to a cockpit winch ■ **266.**

■ **266** *Winching the survivor on board*

■ **267** *Hoisting the survivor on board with a mainsail*

If the survivor is wearing a safety harness

Attach a halyard to it and haul him on board.

If the survivor is weak or injured

Lower a bosun's chair secured to the topping lift or a halyard.

Lower a jib, genoa, or mainsail – removed from its track – into the water. The jib or genoa should be well sheeted home, and a larger genoa is preferable to a small jib ■ **267, 268**

A half inflated dinghy can be thrown in the water and used as an aid.

■ **268** *Hoisting the survivor on board with the genoa*

Getting on board by yourself

Do not try to hoist yourself on board, that is, pull yourself up with your arms.

Go to the lee side.

Take hold of the toe rail or a stanchion, then lean back in the water, kick a heel over the rail or behind a stanchion.

Pull yourself on board with your legs.

NOTE:

When making a passage or sailing single-handed, a line of about 30 metres should be towed behind the boat with a loop and/or a float, such as an empty plastic bottle, on the end ■ **269.**

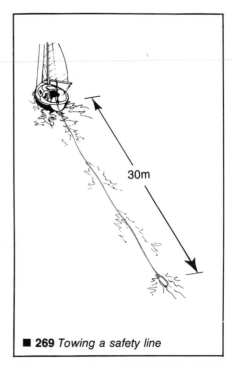

30m

■ **269** *Towing a safety line*

Mast

See: Climbing the mast, Dismasting, Rigging failure

Medical assistance

International Code of Signals

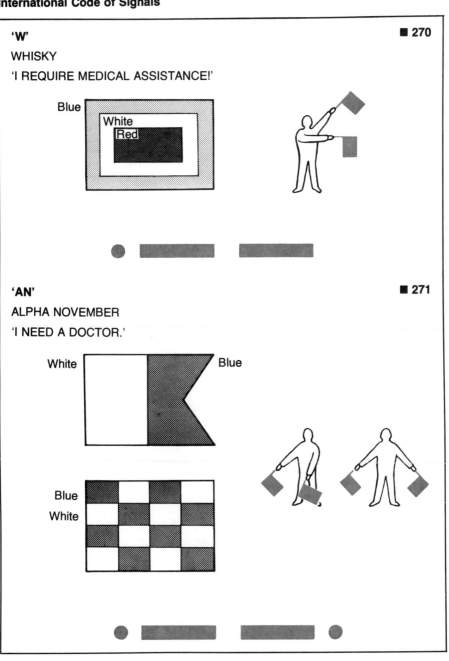

'W' ■ 270
WHISKY
'I REQUIRE MEDICAL ASSISTANCE!'

Blue
White
Red

'AN' ■ 271
ALPHA NOVEMBER
'I NEED A DOCTOR.'

White Blue

Blue
White

Medical emergencies

See: Antibiotics, Antiseptics, Appendicitis, Artificial respiration, Burns, Constipation, Death, Diarrhoea, Ears, Evacuation, Exposure, Eyes, Fatigue, Fish hook injuries, Fractures, Frostbite, Haemorrhages, Heat exhaustion, Immersion foot, Infection, Injections, Medical assistance, Medical kit, Pain-killers, Poisoned fish, Scurvy, Sea-sickness, Shock, Sleeping pills, Sprains, Sterilization, Sunburn, Sunstroke, Toothaches, Tranquillizers, Tropical jelly fish stings, Urine, Vitamins, Water, Wounds

Medical kit

Antibiotics **See: Antibiotics**

Antihistamines **See: Tropical jelly fish stings**

Antiseptics **See: Antiseptics**

Aspirin

Bandages, compresses and water-proof dressings

Burn cream

Burn dressings

Butterfly bandages

Constipation tablets **See: Constipation**

Cotton wool

Cough medicine

Diarrhoea tablets **See: Diarrhoea**

Disposable sterile gloves

Elastic bandages

Epsom salts

Eye drops

Eye ointment

Forceps

Foot powder

Gauze

Indigestion tablets

Milk of Magnesia

Needle, suture and cat-gut

Pain-killers **See: Pain-killers**

Petroleum gauze

Plaster

Safety pins

Scissors

Sea-sickness tablets **See: Sea-sickness**

Splints

Stay-awake tablets **See: Fatigue**

Sticking plasters

Surgical detergent

Suntan oil

Thermometer

Throat lozenges

Tincture of Iodine

Tourniquet

Tranquillizers **See: Tranquillizers**

Vitamins

Wound-dressings

Morse code

Morse Code

A	• ▬	N	▬ •	1 • ▬ ▬ ▬ ▬
B	▬ • • •	O	▬ ▬ ▬	2 • • ▬ ▬ ▬
C	▬ • ▬ •	P	• ▬ ▬ •	3 • • • ▬ ▬
D	▬ • •	Q	▬ ▬ • ▬	4 • • • • ▬
E	•	R	• ▬ •	5 • • • • •
F	• • ▬ •	S	• • •	6 ▬ • • • •
G	▬ ▬ •	T	▬	7 ▬ ▬ • • •
H	• • • •	U	• • ▬	8 ▬ ▬ ▬ • •
I	• •	V	• • • ▬	9 ▬ ▬ ▬ ▬ •
J	• ▬ ▬ ▬	W	• ▬ ▬	0 ▬ ▬ ▬ ▬ ▬
K	▬ • ▬	X	▬ • • ▬	
L	• ▬ • •	Y	▬ • ▬ ▬	
M	▬ ▬	Z	▬ ▬ • •	

Morse code by flags

Separation of dots and/or dashes to mark the end of a letter.

Separation of letters, groups or words.

Erase signal – by the transmitter.
Repeat signal – by the receiver.

Nautical almanac

Out of date

In the back pages of the Almanac, following the year's entries, are instructions which permit the data to be used in the following year. But *only* for the sun and stars.

For the Sun

Use the figures under the same date, but count *back* 5hrs. 48mins. from the G.M.T. of observation. Then add 87° to the G.H.A. found in the Almanac.

For the Stars

Using the same date and time, calculate the G.H.A. and Declination. Then subtract 15° 1′ from the G.H.A. The Declination remains unchanged.

Lost

Sight Reduction Tables HO-249 (AP 3270)

Volume I contains a table from which one can work out the G.H.A. of Aries during the Table's period of validity which is five years from date of issue.

Volumes II and III contain tables for the G.H.A. and Declination of the Sun, valid until the year 2000.

Numbers

	DEUTSCH	ENGLISH	FRANÇAIS	NEDERLANDS	DANSK	ITALIANO	ESPAÑOL	PORTUGUÊS
1	eins	one	un	een	en	uno	uno	um
2	zwei	two	deux	twee	to	due	dos	dois
3	drei	three	trois	drie	tre	tre	tres	três
4	vier	four	quatre	vier	fire	quattro	cuatro	quatro
5	fünf	five	cinq	vijf	fem	cinque	cinco	cinco
6	sechs	six	six	zes	seks	sei	seis	seis
7	sieben	seven	sept	zeven	syv	sette	siete	sete
8	acht	eight	huit	acht	otte	otto	ocho	oito
9	neun	nine	neuf	negen	ni	nove	nueve	nove
10	zehn	ten	dix	tien	ti	dieci	diez	dez
11	elf	eleven	onze	elf	elleve	undici	once	onze
12	zwölf	twelve	douze	twaalf	tolv	dodici	doce	doze
13	dreizehn	thirteen	treize	dertien	tretten	tredici	trece	treze
14	vierzehn	fourteen	quatorze	veertien	fjorten	quattordici	catorce	catorze
15	fünfzehn	fifteen	quinze	vijftien	femten	quindici	quince	quinze
16	sechzehn	sixteen	seize	zestien	seksten	sedici	dieciséis	dezaseis
17	siebzehn	seventeen	dix-sept	zeventien	sytten	diciassette	diecisiete	dezasete
18	achtzehn	eighteen	dix-huit	achttien	atten	diciotto	dieciocho	dezoito
19	neunzehn	nineteen	dix-neuf	~~digentien~~	nitten	diciannove	diecinueve	dezanove
20	zwanzig	twenty	vingt	twintig	tyve	venti	veinte	vinte
30	dreißig	thirty	trente	dertig	tredive	trenta	treinta	trinta
40	vierzig	forty	quarante	veertig	fyrre	quaranta	cuaranta	quarenta
50	fünfzig	fifty	cinquante	vijftig	halvtreds	cinquanta	cincuenta	cinquenta
60	sechzig	sixty	soixante	zestig	tres	sessanta	sesenta	sessenta
70	siebzig	seventy	soixante-dix	zeventig	halvfjerds	settanta	setenta	setenta
80	achtzig	eighty	quatre-vingt	tachtig	firs	ottanta	ochenta	oitenta
90	neunzig	ninety	quatre-vingt-dix	negentig	halvfems	novanta	noventa	noventa
100	einhundert	one hundred	cent	honderd	hundrede	cento	cient	cem
1000	tausend	thousand	mille	duizend	tusind	mille	mil	mil

O

Oil

Pouring oil onto the sea can be advantageous in certain situations:

Manoeuvring alongside another boat in heavy weather.

Hove-to in heavy weather.

Passing through a stretch of heavy surf.

Crossing a bar.

Type and amount

The most effective kinds of oil are animal, vegetable or fish oils. Failing those, lubricating oil should be used.

As a rough guide, one litre of heavy oil will cover approximately 20 square metres, that is, about the deck space of two yachts. In a bad sea releasing small amounts of oil may not offer much relief.

Principle

A heavy, low viscosity oil will float on the surface of the sea and spread out into a thin film with a high tensile strength. This produces an often extraordinary calming effect – but *only* on the tendency of waves to crest and break. It will *not* in any way reduce their size.

NOTE:

Often the problem with releasing oil is that the boat and the oil slick may drift at different rates.

Oil bags ■ 272, 273, 274, 275, 276

Fill a plastic container ½ to ¾ full of heavy oil.

Wrap it in several layers of old rags ■ 272.

Sew it into a canvas bag.

Just before using, puncture the container several times with a marlin spike ■ 273.

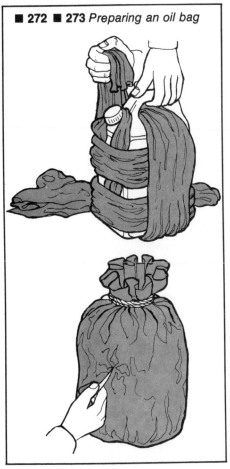

■ 272 ■ 273 *Preparing an oil bag*

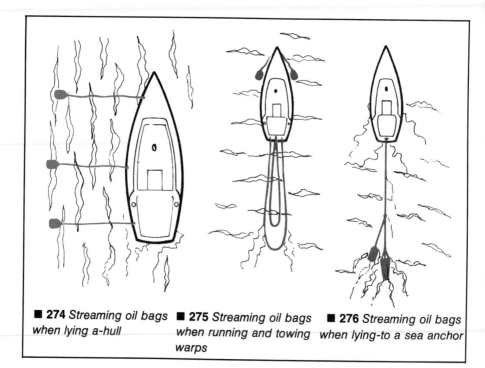

■ **274** *Streaming oil bags when lying a-hull*   ■ **275** *Streaming oil bags when running and towing warps*   ■ **276** *Streaming oil bags when lying-to a sea anchor*

If lying a-hull

Stream the bags to windward ■ **274.**

If running and towing warps

Stream the bags from the bow ■ **275.**

If lying to a sea anchor

Stream the bags from the sea anchor ■ **276.**

Oil hose ■ 277

Fill a length of old plastic hose, 4–5cm. in diameter with oil and seal both ends.

Tie a buoyancy aid – plastic bottle, fender, life-jacket or lifering – to the outer end.

Puncture the hose as it is streamed over the side.

Tow it at least 10 metres behind the boat.

Pumping out oil

Oil can be pumped out of a windward sea-cock, such as a toilet or sink drain, or simply poured into the bilge and discharged by a bilge pump.

NOTE:

For swimming in an oily sea **See: Abandon ship!**

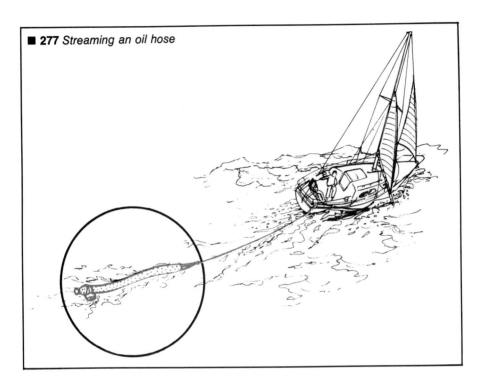

■ **277** *Streaming an oil hose*

P

Pain-killers

Pain-killers are known as analgesics, drugs that relieve pain without producing loss of consciousness. Narcotics depress the brain cells involved in pain perception and to some extent affect a person's sensations of pain. Synthetic narcotics usually encourage relaxation, but may cause constipation.

NOTE:

Do *not* use narcotics for head injuries. Narcotics are respiratory depressants.

England

	Moderate Pain-killers Dosage
Aspirin	600mg. or 2 tablets 4 times/day
Distalgesic	1 tablet 4 times/ day
Paracetamol	2 tablets every 4 hours
	Strong Pain-killers Dosage
Codeine	30–60mg. 3 times/ day

France

	Dosage
Aspirine	500mg. or 2 tablets 4 times/day
Diantalvic	1 tablet 4 times/ day
Dolipren	2 tablets every 4 hours
	Strong Pain-killers Dosage
Codeine	30–60mg. 3 times/ day

Germany

	Dosage
Aspirin	600mg. 2 tablets 4 times/day
Novalgin	1 tablet 4 times/ day
Ben-u-ron	1–2 tablets 2–3 times/ day
	Strong Pain-killers Dosage
Eukodal	$\frac{1}{2}$ tablet once/ day

NOTE:

Aspirin can be surprisingly effective when used in conjunction with Codeine.

Dosage: 600mg. Aspirin and 30mg. Codeine every four hours.

Petrol Engine

See: Engine Failure, Petrol

Pilot

International Code of Signals

'G'
GOLF
'I REQUIRE A PILOT.'

For light patterns of pilot
vessels **See: Lights**

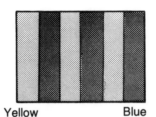

Yellow   Blue

■ 278

 ● ● ● ●   **Pilot vessel on duty**

Pilot vessel making way

2 minutes   2 minutes

Pilot vessel stopped but not at anchor

2 minutes   2 minutes

Pilot vessel at anchor

   1 minute   1 minute
4 short blasts   4 short blasts
5 seconds   5 seconds

Poisoned fish

See also: Fish

Unfortunately, in tropical waters nearly any fish worth eathing – mullet, eel, herring, shark, turtle, shellfish, etc. – *can* be poisoned, and there appears to be no way of knowing beforehand whether or not a fish is contaminated.

One thing is clear: the phenomenon is regional, to such an extent that fish on one side of a lagoon or bay can be poisoned and on the other side be completely healthy. Before fishing in coastal waters or lagoons it is often wise to seek local advice.

When in doubt

Do not eat the viscera – heart, liver, etc.

Eat smaller varieties of fish, those of less than 1 kg.

Soak the cleaned, filleted fish in fresh water for at least an hour, changing the water several times.

If poisoned

Immediately induce vomiting by:

Sticking a finger down your throat.

or

Drinking a solution of two teaspoons salt in a glass of water.

Take three tablespoons of olive oil to induce diarrhoea.

Then seek local aid for an antidote.

Pole star

See: Stars

Propellers

If a line becomes wound around the propeller ■ 279, 280

First, bring end on deck. Put the engine in neutral, turn it over by hand, and try to unwind the line.

If it must be cut

For coils of wire or cable *only* a hacksaw and new blade will be effective.

For tightly wound and compressed ropes a hacksaw is best, but an old knife with a chipped blade or a breadknife will also be effective.

Procedure

If the boat is of light displacement, shifting weight to the bow, such as that of the crew, can raise the propeller closer to the surface where it will be easier to work on ■ 279.

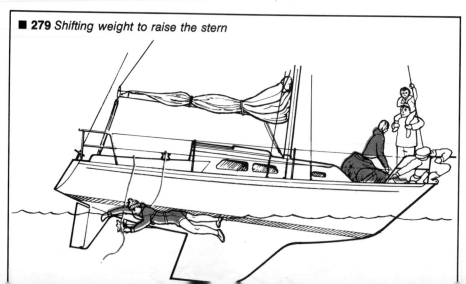

■ **279** *Shifting weight to raise the stern*

An inflatable dinghy, half inflated and capsized, can make an excellent working platform ■ **280.**

A face mask and/or snorkel can make the task easier.

Tools should be secured with lines so that both hands can be free to fend off the boat.

WARNING:

When working over the side, wear a safety harness.

Also, for protection against barnacle scrapes, a shirt, gloves and woolly hat.

A kapok or cork life-jacket tied around your head will offer some protection against a bouncing stern.

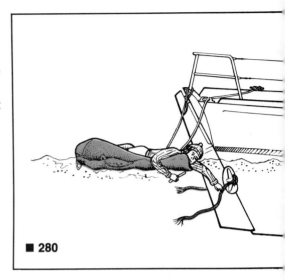

■ **280**

Pumps

The engine's water pump as a bilge pump ■ 281, 282

Close the water intake sea-cock.

Remove the hose and place it in the bilge. An extra length of hose may need to be added.

If possible, place a piece of screen or fine net over the end as these pumps are susceptible to clogging.

Start the engine.

WARNING:

Engine cooling pumps are not high capacity pumps. Engines of 10–50 h.p. normally deliver only 20–90 litres per minute, less than that of a manual bilge pump. However, since it can be an extra hand, a permanent system with a switch can easily be installed ■ **282.**

For the capacities of different kinds of pumps See: Holes

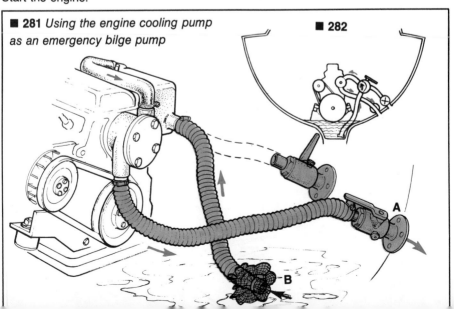

■ **281** *Using the engine cooling pump as an emergency bilge pump*

■ **282**

A

B

R

Radar reflectors

Mounting

The best location is at the masthead.

Failing that, the reflector should be secured:
In a stable position.
As high as possible.
Where it will not be blanketed by metal spars or wet sails.

An octahedral reflector should *not* be mounted in a point-up attitude, rather so that its base remains in a flat box-like or 'catch-rain' position ■ **283.**

The surfaces must be kept clean and free from corrosion.

■ **283** *A radar reflector mounted in the correct 'catch rain' position*

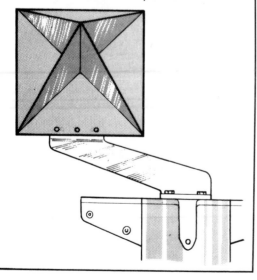

NOTE:

The smallest commercial reflector properly mounted four metres above the deck will return a strong echo to a ship five miles away.

WARNING:

1 – Bits or strips of aluminium foil, biscuit tins, jerry cans, or other metallic garbage hoisted aloft can be considered worthless. Also metal spars and masts are not substitutes, as a mast would only return a signal if the boat were not heeled.

2 – In conditions of bad weather and visibility you are less likely to be detected at extremely close range than farther out. Also rain and snow tend to reduce the reflector's effectiveness.

Principle

A radar reflector is nothing more than a set of metal mirrors, aligned at 90 degree angles, so that a beam striking one of them is reflected on to the next until it is finally returned to the source along the same path as it came. For this reason, it is absolutely essential that the plates be positioned at perfect right angles. An error of a few degrees can reduce the effectiveness of a reflector by as much as half.

The larger the reflector, the more beams returned. Since effectiveness increases with area, a reflector 50cm. a side is about five times more effective than a 30cm. one.

Radio direction finder

Homing

Place the ferrite aerial of the unit parallel with the fore and aft line of the boat. Swing the boat until the unit registers a 'null' – the point of weakest reception. Read the course from the boat's compass.

WARNING:

1 – Bearings taken an hour before to an hour after sunrise or sunset should be regarded as suspect due to 'Night Effect' – a tendency of the ionosphere to change its properties at those times.

2 – Steel or aluminium boats may have unpredictable errors. These can be minimized by always taking bearing from the same location on board.

3 – If the bearing of a radio beacon makes an acute angle with the coast, it may be slightly deflected. The error – usually not more than five degrees – will be in the direction of the coast.

NOTE:

When three or more bearings result in a 'cocked hat', your position is more than likely:

A – Within the triangle ■ **284.**

B – Closer to the shorter sides – 'The shorter, the closer' ■ **285.**

■ 284

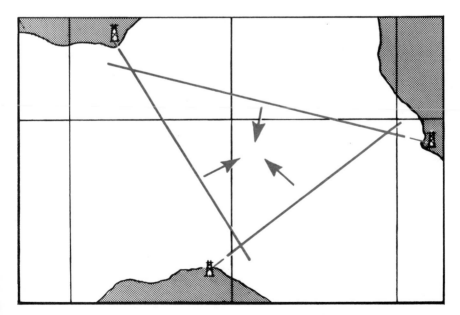

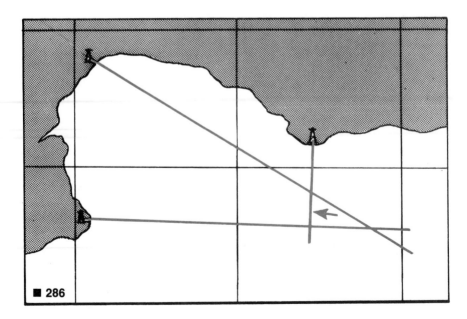

■ 285

C – Closer to the bearing with the
smallest distance to range ratio, that is,
the bearing which has the smallest

$$\frac{\text{approximate distance to beacon}}{\text{Beacon Range}}$$ ■ 286.

■ 286

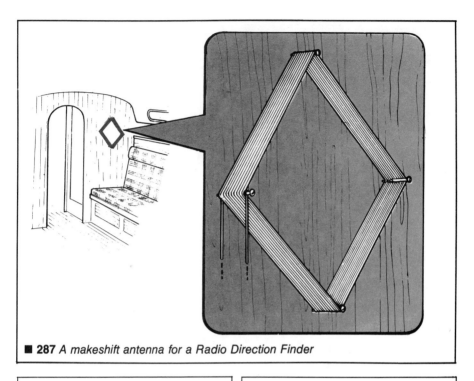

■ **287** *A makeshift antenna for a Radio Direction Finder*

A makeshift antenna ■ 287

Rainwater

Collecting rainwater at sea

Materials

Twenty-five metres of insulated wire

Four large screws

Procedure

On an athwartship bulkhead, place the screws in a square about 60cm. on a side.

Begin at the bottom and wind the wire around the square about 10 times, ending in the same position you began.

Attach the two leads to the receiver's loop connection.

Tune in a strong station, then *swing the boat* to find the null point, that is, the point of weakest reception.

The bearing to the station can be read from the boat's compass.

METHOD 1

Hang a bucket near the gooseneck, but wait a few minutes for the salt to wash off the mainsail. Raising the topping lift can greatly increase the flow ■ **288.**

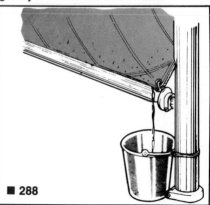

■ **288**

METHOD 2

Tie a pre-prepared plastic sheet between the shrouds, but leave enough extra line at the corners so that it can be adjusted to face the wind ■ **289.**

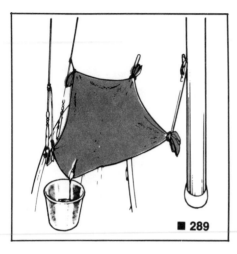

■ **289**

METHOD 3

Lash two spars or oars together and fasten the plastic sheet between them ■ **290.**

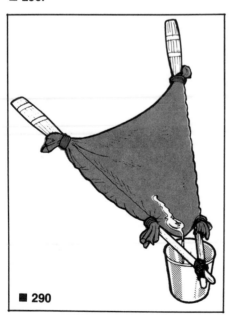

■ **290**

Collecting rainwater at anchor

METHOD 1

Construct a rain collecting sheet from plastic or the sun awning with a hole in the centre which is joined to a piece of plastic hose. Tie the sheet between the shrouds and run the tubing into the tank, or a jerry can ■ **291.**

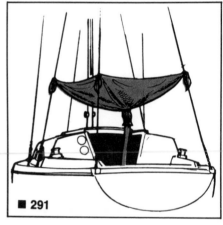

■ **291**

METHOD 2

Construct gutters for the coach roof by cutting a few metres of plastic tubing lengthwise ■ **292.**

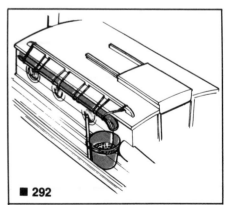

■ **292**

METHOD 3

Cover the cockpit with a sail, fastened to the coachroof and lifelines and allow it to drain into a bucket on the floor of the cockpit ■ 293.

NOTE:

In emergencies, dry clothes or towels can be laid on the deck then wrung into a bucket later.

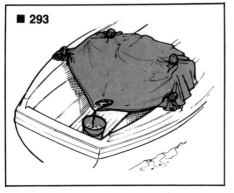

■ 293

Reefing and sail reduction

See also: Heavy weather

The moment to reduce sail

If going to windward or reaching, when

the boat is heeling over too far.
The boat is moving too fast for the seas.
The sails are too light for the wind.
The motion of the boat has become uncomfortable.

If the boat is running it is easy to have a false sense of security and a false estimation of wind and sea speed.

As a general rule, never carry more sail while running than would be carried while beating or reaching.

Principle

Wind force – thrust – increases 2–3 times faster than speed. Thus, reduction in sail does not necessarily mean a reduction in speed.

Procedure

As the weather becomes worse, low cut headsails should be replaced by high cut ones to prevent possible damage from the sea or wind.

The centre of effort, that is, the sail area centre, should be lowered and moved forward amidships.

For the safety of the main mast, some sail should be left on to prevent whipping in high seas.

Revolving storms

See: Law of storms

Rigging failures

Emergency action

Should any part of the standing rigging – shrouds, forestays, backstays, the hounds, a bottlescrew, or the cable – part or show signs of parting:

If the seas are calm

Take down all sail at once.

If the seas are rough

It is better to continue sailing than to risk the strain which might be put on the mast by rolling and pitching in the waves, even with a sea anchor streamed from the bow or stern.

If a shroud has parted

More than likely it will be the weather one.

Go immediately on to the other tack, and bring the wind abeam. At that point the rigging will again be at near normal strength.

WARNING:

Gybing can be dangerous, especially with a flexible mast. Generally, the few seconds gained are not worth the risk.

If a forestay has parted

Turn downwind so that the strain of the mast is placed on the backstay. Depending on weather conditions, a full headsail will also relieve some of the tension.

If a backstay has parted

Bring the boat up into the wind.

Drop the headsails.

If the boat has running backstays, set up the leeward one as well.

If a bottle screw has given way

Remove the broken bottle screw, attach a new piece of rigging wire to the deck fitting.

Form the other end into a bight with bulldog clamps and connect it to the existing wire by means of:

1 – A block and tackle. **See: Block and tackle**

2 – A lanyard. **See: Lanyard**

3 – Another bottlescrew ■ **294.**

4 – A lashing ■ **295.**

If a splice has given way

Bend the broken end of the wire to form an eye which can be either spliced or held in place with bulldog clamps. **See: Bulldog clamps**

If the bottle screw will open

Open it, and connect it to the new eye in the cable by means of:

1 – Another bottlescrew ■ **296.**

2 – A chain of shackles ■ **297.**

3 – A length of chain with a shackle on each end ■ **298.**

4 – A lashing.

Take up the slack with the bottlescrew.

If the bottle screw will not open

Attach one end of a strong piece of cord to the eye of the wire and the other to a shackle fixed to the bottlescrew.

Insert a marlin spike or screwdriver between the strands, and rotating it, like a Spanish windlass, to take up the slack ■ **299.** Use wrenches or screwdrivers to prevent the bottle screw and eye from twisting.

When the wire is taut, join the eye to the shackle with a chain of shackles, lashing or lanyard.

See: Lanyard

If one or more strands of wire has broken

Lay another piece of wire alongside it, stretch it as tightly as possible, then clamp it in place with bulldog clamps. **See: Bulldog clamps**

Tape the loose ends to protect the sails ■ **300.**

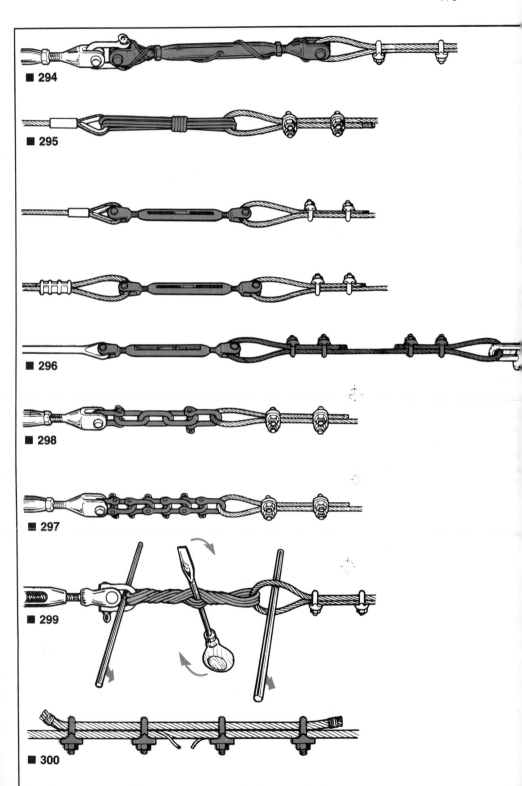

■ 294

■ 295

■ 296

■ 298

■ 297

■ 299

■ 300

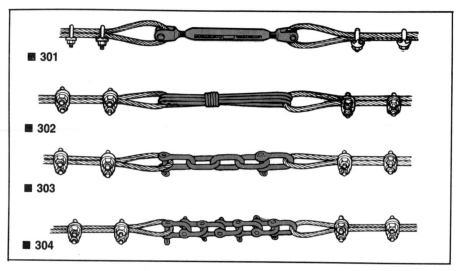

■ 301
■ 302
■ 303
■ 304

If a cable has broken

Bend both ends of the cable into eyes and fasten them with bulldog clamps. **See: Bulldog clamps**

Join the two eyes together with:
A bottle screw ■ **301.**
A strong lashing ■ **302.**
A short length of chain ■ **303.**
A chain of shackles ■ **304.**

Take up the slack with the bottle screw.

Cutting wire rope or cable ■ 305

With wire cutters

Make a whipping 3cm. on either side of the cutting point. Whip away from the cutting point. Then use the wire cutters.

With a cold chisel

Make a whipping 3cm. on either side of the cutting point.

Place the wire on a hard surface such as a steel blade, anchor winch, big hammer or deck fitting.

Strike the wire a few times to flatten it.

Hold the chisel on the surface and slowly cut the strands.

■ 305 *Cutting wire rope or cable*

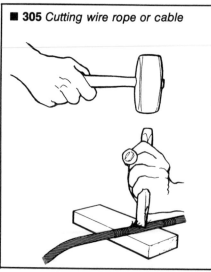

Temporary repair of a shroud or the forestay

METHOD 1 ■ 306

Shackle a free foresail halyard to the chain plate or the forestay fitting. If there is no place to attach the shackle, the connection must be made with a lashing.

Take up the slack on the halyard winch

until the line is taut. Although the halyard will probably bear an enormous amount of strain, it is still no replacement for the wire and therefore should not be set up too tightly.

METHOD 2 ■ 307

Shackle a free halyard to the forestay fitting, and tie a length of line to the other end.

Attach a block to the forestay fitting and run the line through the block, then on to the halyard winch.

METHOD 3 ■ 308

If the halyards are in the mast, or unavailable, and the break is at a reachable height, then quick repair can be made with a small block and tackle and bulldog clamps.

Make an eye in the long end of the shroud or forestay with bulldog clamps. **See: Bulldog clamps**

or

Tie on end of the block and tackle to the cable with a rolling hitch **(See: Knots)** 15–20cm. above the break. Below that, fasten a bulldog clamp to the cable to prevent the knot from sliding.

The other end of the block and tackle can be secured to a fitting.

NOTE:

This method saves the use of a halyard.

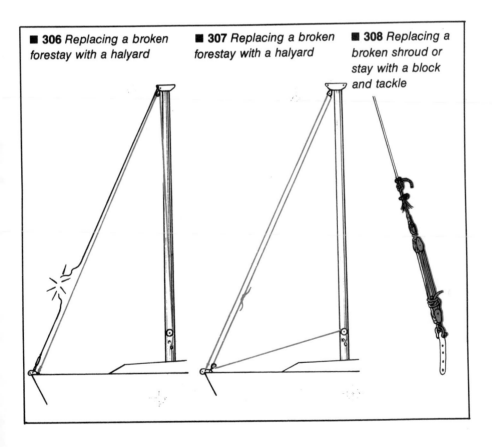

■ **306** *Replacing a broken forestay with a halyard*

■ **307** *Replacing a broken forestay with a halyard*

■ **308** *Replacing a broken shroud or stay with a block and tackle*

Temporary repair of the backstay ■ 309

METHOD 1

Shackle the topping lift to the backstay fitting.

Attach some line to the other end, and take up the slack on the halyard winch.

METHOD 2 ■ 310

If the boat has a long boom, the mast can be securely supported by leaving the topping lift shackled to the boom.

Tie the free end of the topping lift to the outhaul fitting on the end of the boom. It may be necessary to add a length of line.

Draw up the slack and support the mast with the mainsheet.

NOTE:

On modern boats with short booms, the mast may be given additional support by shackling a foresail or spinnaker halyard to the backstay fitting. This will probably involve twisting or bending the masthead block into place, as well as chafing the line, but this may be necessary to prevent further damage.

METHOD 3 ■ 311

If the boat is without a topping lift and a halyard winch as well, the foresail halyard is cleated home to the mast, and bit of extra line attached to the other end which is taken aft, run through a block, on the backstay fitting and then on to a cockpit winch.

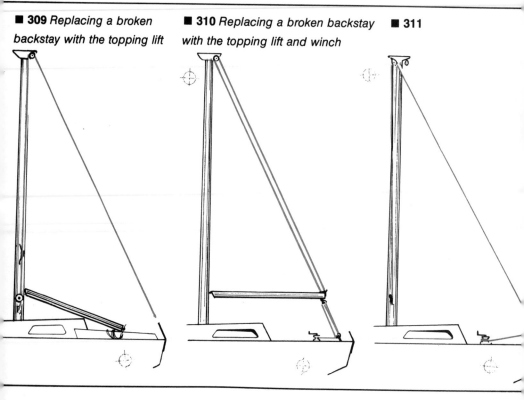

■ **309** *Replacing a broken backstay with the topping lift*

■ **310** *Replacing a broken backstay with the topping lift and winch*

■ **311**

Right of way
See: Collision

Running

Purpose

When sea and wind conditions no longer permit the boat to remain hove-to, the decision must be made to run with the storm.

The boat then rides with the wind and seas, and the relative wind and wave speeds are reduced. However, unless the waves are extremely short, the boat will never move at the same speed as the waves. Being pooped and broaching will always be a danger.

Way is kept on, which allows the boat to be steered and to compensate for dangerous cross-seas. How much way – that is, the speed of the boat to be maintained – is a highly debatable subject which is dependent upon the special characteristics of the storm, waves and boat. In general, the shorter the waves, the slower the boat's speed should be. When in doubt, err on the side of slowing down.

The three basic tactics for running

Running under reduced sail.
Running under bare poles.
Running while streaming warps.

WARNING:

When running, the weakest parts of the boat – stern, cockpit and after cabin bulkhead – are presented to the seas. Never leave the companionway open, and always keep the cockpit drains clear.

Running under reduced sail

Take the seas dead astern or slightly on the quarter which will lead you away from the storm centre.

The boat should not carry more sail when running than when beating into the storm.

Usually, the guide for when to reduce sail further is the size of the seas, rather than the strength of the wind.

The last sail to come off is the staysail or jib sheeted flat to the mast. **See: Reefing and sail reduction**

Running under bare poles

All sail is taken down, the mainsail stripped from the boom, and the sail bags stowed below.

The boat is steered, and thus takes each wave as it comes.

Even stripped of all sails, the boat will still have considerable windage due to her freeboard, mast and rigging, and hence can make considerable speed. If the speed is too great, warps may have to be streamed.

Running while streaming warps ■ 312

This will greatly reduce the forward movement of the boat. The distinction between streaming warps and streaming a sea anchor is that the former breaks or retards the boat's speed, while the latter tends to stop her.

Streaming warps will help the boat keep her stern into the wind and also have a quieting effect on the seas astern.

WARNING:

If the warps cause an excessive strain they may rob the boat of some of her buoyancy. **See: Sea anchor**

Procedure

The warps may be streamed from either quarter, tied in a bight, or fastened to a bridle. They should be well secured to

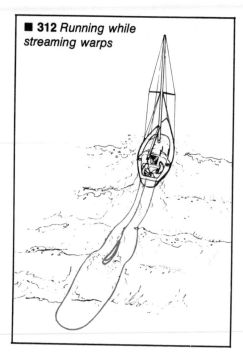

■ 312 *Running while streaming warps*

deck fittings or cockpit winches as the strain can be enormous.

The warps should be as thick as possible.

Knots can be tied to increase the drag.

The length will have to be adjusted to the sea and wind conditions. Normally, between 80 and 250 metres of warp is required.

More than one warp can be streamed.

Single warps with such items as liferings, fenders, tyres, or sailbags tied to the ends can also be used.

More than likely the boat will still need to be steered.

Rules of the road

See: Collision

S

Safety harness

Points

Points to clip on to

Jackstays

Shrouds

Lifelines

Pin rail

Points which can be dangerous to clip on to (as they can trip the snap hook open)

Stanchion bases with welded legs

Chainplates

Pulpit

Pushpit

Eye bolts

Deck fittings

Points *not* to clip on to

Deck cleats

Mast cleats

Wooden handrails

Bottlescrews

NOTE:

Looping the safety line around the fitting and clipping the hook on to the line will greatly reduce the strength of the line.

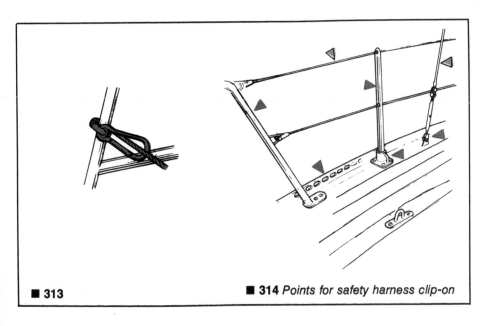

■ 313

■ 314 *Points for safety harness clip-on*

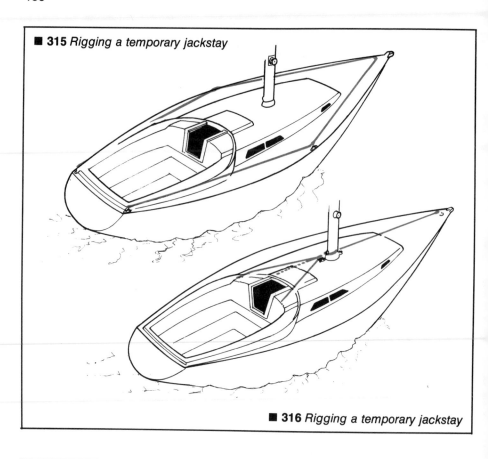

■ **315** *Rigging a temporary jackstay*

■ **316** *Rigging a temporary jackstay*

A temporary jackstay ■ 315, 316

Use strong rope or wire cable.

Run a line lengthwise on each side of the boat, shackling it securely to deck fittings.

If necessary, a single or double line will serve – from the bow, to the mast, over the coach roof, then to the cockpit.

Always clip on *before* leaving the cockpit

Sailing astern

For downwind berthing stern-to, or coming out of irons

Leave the mainsheet slack, and back the jib. In small boats it is preferable to back

the mainsail instead ■ **317.**

Point the rudder in the *opposite direction* to that in which you wish the bow to turn ■ **318.**

Sail reduction

See: Reefing

Sail repair

Tears and rips ■ 319

Materials

Thread.

Needles.

Beeswax.

Sewing palm.

Procedure

Double, even quadruple, the thread.

Wax the thread by drawing it several times across the beeswax.

Make a knot in the end and sew using a sailmaker's darn (herringbone stitch).

Make 5–6 stitches per 2.5cm.

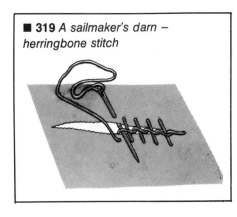

■ **319** *A sailmaker's darn – herringbone stitch*

Any tear longer than 5cm. which is not along a seam should be patched.

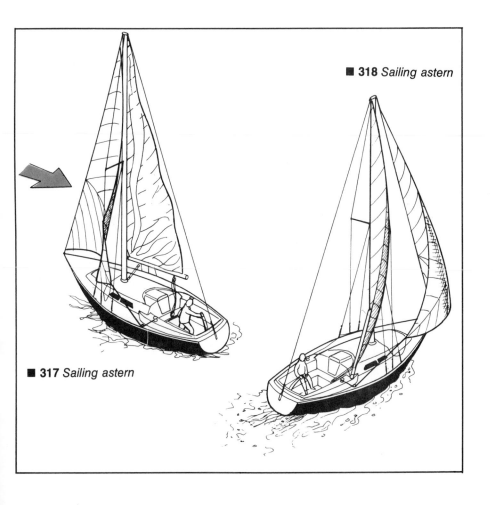

■ **318** *Sailing astern*

■ **317** *Sailing astern*

Patching ■ 320, 321, 322

Materials

Thread.

Needles.

Beeswax.

Sewing palm.

Patch: this should be approximately the same weight cloth as the sail being repaired. It should be large enough to extend 5cm. on either side of the tear.

Procedure

If possible, sew the break closed with an overhand stitch ■ **320.**

If the patch is cut from a synthetic fabric, hot seal the edges with an iron, soldering iron, or screwdriver heated on the stove. Failing that, turn the edges under.

If the patch is cut from canvas, turn the edges under.

Place the patch on the sail with its warp and weft lined up with that of the sail.

Hold the patch in place by means of tape, pins, or stitches in the corners ■ **321.**

Sew the patch on with an overhand or seam stitch ■ **322.**

WARNING:

Even though Terylene sails are harder and will take more punishment than canvas, the seams of synthetic fabrics are highly vulnerable. Whereas stitches in cotton or flax tend to sink in and become a part of the cloth, stitches in Terylene stand out, and if too large a thread is used, make little holes of their own. For this reason, three rows of stitches on a seam are required. The two outer ones will hopefully protect the inner one.

For tears along the bolt rope ■ 323

Wrap the patch around the bolt rope, then sew it through from both sides and along the edge of the rope.

Patching a sail

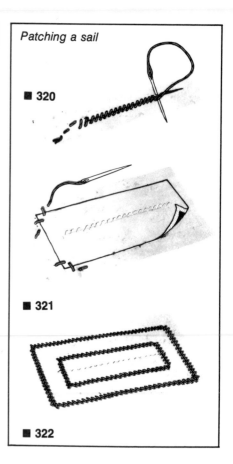

■ 320

■ 321

■ 322

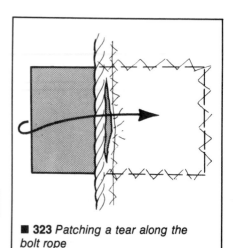

■ **323** *Patching a tear along the bolt rope*

For tears along the headboard
■ 324

Fold a large patch over the headboard which covers the tear on both sides. Stitch along the base of the headboard, fold in the flaps of the patch, then sew through the headboard holes.

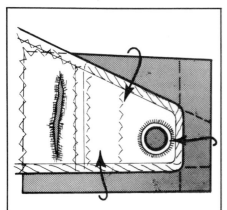

■ **324** *Patching a tear along the headboard*

For tears along a batten pocket ■ 325

Remove the stitches along the edge of the pocket and slide in the patch. Sew the patch on, then re-sew the pocket in place.

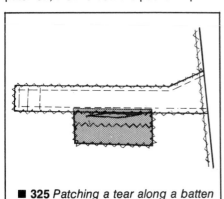

■ **325** *Patching a tear along a batten pocket*

For tears at the tack or clew

METHOD 1

Sew in a round thimble, install the liner, then flare out the edges ■ **326.**

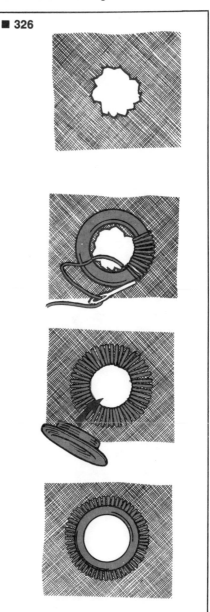

■ **326**

METHOD 2

Sew a piece of rope around the hole ■ 327 either around the rope or, if possible, through it.

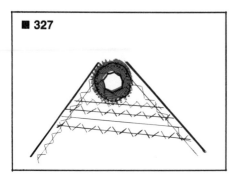

■ 327

METHOD 3

Make a rope cringle around the bolt rope. This can be fabricated as shown from a length of (■ 328) strong line.

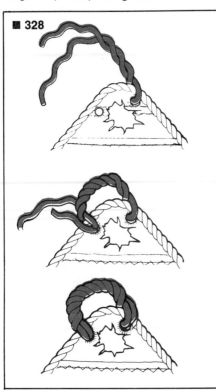

■ 328

METHOD 4

Sew a shackle, either over the hole or to the bolt rope which will serve as a sheet point ■ **329.**

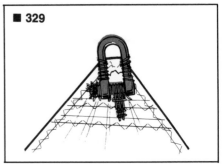

■ 329

NOTE:

To reduce stress, pass the sheet several times through the clew, then secure it with a bowline.

METHOD 5

Fold the clew several times, bunch the sail together and lash it securely ■ **330.**

Long tears, blown-out sails and weakened sailcloth

Materials

A strong, water-resistant contact glue.

Patching material. If not enough is available, a sailbag makes a good substitute.

Procedure

Clean the glueing surfaces with fresh water and let them dry.

If the break is along a seam, don't use a patch.

Spread the glue evenly on both surfaces and let it nearly dry.

Press the two surfaces together.

To make a solid bond, pound the entire joint with a block of wood and a hammer.

■ 330

For easy sewing

Lay the sail and patch over a cutting board across your knees, and place the seam along the edge.

Hold the sail taut by means of a shock cord and hook **■ 331.**

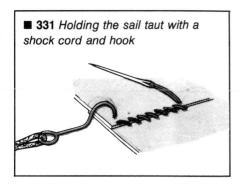

■ 331 *Holding the sail taut with a shock cord and hook*

For fast sewing on heavy cloth

Hold the sail vertically, and with a man on either side, each armed with a sewing palm and a pair of pliers, push and pull the needles back and forth.

Chafe

On the seams

Cover both sides of the seam with sail tape (nylon or Terylene) and stitch it lightly in place.

On sails

Once a chafe mark appears, cover the area on *both* sides with a patch of light Terylene.

Prevention

Rig a boom vang so that the sail will lose its tendency to ride up and down on the shrouds and spreaders.

Cover spreader ends with tape, a leather bag or tennis balls.

Cover turnbuckles with tape, plastic hose, or rags.

See: Baggywrinkle

Salvage

Misconceptions

The acceptance of a tow-line from another boat does not *automatically* entitle them to claim salvage.

The acceptance of aid from a crew member of another boat does not *automatically* entitle him to claim salvage.

A salvor does not *automatically* become the owner of the property he rescues.

Principle

By law and custom sailors are bound to do everything in their power to help save lives at sea, but they are not obligated to save property.

There is no legal parallel ashore.

For example, should a man in a volunteer fire brigade help put out a fire in your house, he will have no legal claim on your property. However, if he puts out a fire on your boat which is afloat in the harbour he could well be entitled to a salvage award.

To make a valid claim a salvor must show:

The ship was in peril.

His decision to come to the aid – of the property – was voluntary.

He risked his own life and/or property to save the ship.

His efforts were successful.

The degree of the ship's peril, the extent of the salvor's risk, his time, effort, ultimate success, plus the value of the property saved are important factors which a court will use to determine the amount of a salvage award.

Crew members and passengers of a ship generally do not receive salvage awards for saving their vessel.

Salvage agreements

If the captain of a ship in peril comes to an agreement with a salvor beforehand,

that person will have no further salvage rights. A legal contract – such as an agreement for a tow made in the presence of witnesses – takes precedence over a salvage claim.

Often this contract is in the form of the *Lloyd's Open Agreement* which is based on a 'No cure – No pay' arrangement which leaves the amount of the award to be settled later by arbitration. The Lloyd's agreement need not be signed. A verbal accord, such as that hailed between two ships in front of witnesses, is sufficient and binding.

Sculling

When necessary even a boat of 10 metres or more can be sculled short distances in calm waters.

The oar must be securely lashed or fitted in a rowlock or notch in the transom.

It need not be on the centreline of the boat. For example, on double-enders the oar can be lashed to a stern quarter.

Technique ■ 332

Stand facing aft.

Hold the shaft of the oar with both hands.

The blade should be at an angle of about 30 degrees to the transom.

Push the oar to one side so that the blade digs into the water.

Twist your wrist to turn the blade back to an angle of 30 degrees.

Then repeat the process – push and twist – push and twist.

LLOYD'S

NOTES.

1. Insert name of person signing on behalf of owners of property to be salved. The Master should sign wherever possible.

2. The Contractor's name should always be inserted in line 3 and whenever the Agreement is signed by the Master of the Salving vessel or other person on behalf of the Contractor the name of the Master or other person must also be inserted in line 3 before the words " for and on behalf of ". The words " for and on behalf of " should be deleted where a Contractor signs personally.

STANDARD FORM OF

SALVAGE AGREEMENT

(APPROVED AND PUBLISHED BY THE COMMITTEE OF LLOYD'S)

NO CURE——NO PAY

On board the

Dated   19

See Note 1 above IT IS HEREBY AGREED between Captain†   for and on behalf of the Owners of the "   " her cargo and freight and   for and on behalf of See Note 2 above (hereinafter called "the Contractor" *):—

1. The Contractor agrees to use his best endeavours to salve the   and/or her cargo and take them into   or other place to be hereafter agreed. The services shall be rendered and accepted as salvage services upon the principle of "no cure—no pay". In case of arbitration being claimed the Contractor's remuneration in the event of success shall be fixed by arbitration in London in the manner hereinafter prescribed: and any difference arising out of this Agreement or the operations thereunder shall be referred to arbitration in the same way. In the event of the services referred to in this Agreement or any part of such services having been already rendered at the date of this Agreement by the Contractor to the said vessel and/or her cargo it is agreed that the provisions of this Agreement shall apply to such services.

2. The Contractor may make reasonable use of the vessel's gear anchors chains and other appurtenances during and for the purpose of the operations free of expense but shall not unnecessarily damage abandon or sacrifice the same or any other of the property the subject of this Agreement.

3. The Master or other person signing this Agreement on behalf of the property to be salved is not authorised to make or give and the Contractor shall not demand or take any payment draft or order for or on account of the remuneration.

PROVISIONS AS TO SECURITY

4. The Contractor shall immediately after the termination of the services or sooner notify the Committee of Lloyd's of the amount for which he requires security (inclusive of costs, expenses and interest) to be given. Unless otherwise agreed by the parties such security shall be given to the Committee of Lloyd's, and security so given shall be in a form approved by the Committee and shall be given by persons firms or corporations resident in the United Kingdom either satisfactory to the Committee of Lloyd's or agreed by the Contractor. The Committee of Lloyd's shall not be responsible for the sufficiency (whether in amount or otherwise) of any security which shall be given nor for the default or insolvency of any person firm or corporation giving the same.

5. Pending the completion of the security as aforesaid, the Contractor shall have a maritime lien on the property salved for his remuneration. The salved property shall

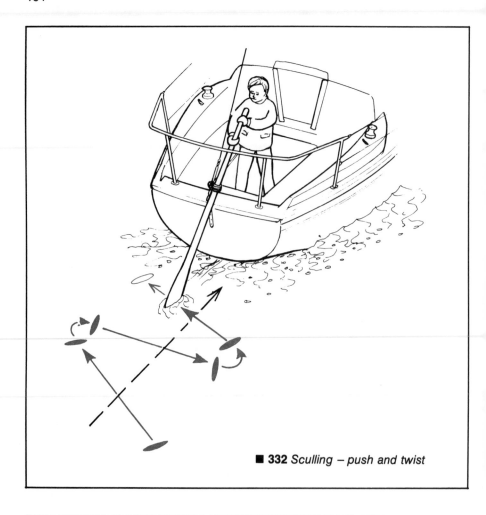

■ **332** *Sculling – push and twist*

Scurvy

Symptoms

Listlessness, fatigue, and a lack of endurance.

Shortness of breath.

Aches and pains in the joints or muscles, particularly at night.

In later stages:
Gums begin to bleed.
Haemorrhages occur in the muscles and joints.

Scars break open.
Wounds refuse to heal.

Medication

Vitamin 'C' – a minimum of 19mg. daily.

NOTE:

Although limes are the traditional preventative on long passages, lemons have substantially more anti-scorbutic value. At sea, 500mg. of vitamin 'C' daily is sufficient to prevent the disease.

Scuttling

If aground in surf, swells or heavy weather and in danger of being broken up, as a last resort the boat must be flooded ■ 333.

Set the best anchors seaward.
See: Anchoring

Run lines ashore to hold the boat in position as securely as possible, so that she will neither be driven further ashore, nor be carried out to sea.

Use floorboards, doors, tabletops, spars or driftwood as wedges to protect the hull as much as possible.

Open all sea-cocks, portholes and hatchways.

Abandon ship.

As the tide recedes, or the weather turns fair, water will drain from the open sea-cocks and there should be a chance to refloat the boat on the next calm, high tide.

NOTE:
Before abandoning ship, strip the boat of all valuable gear.

Sea anchors

In heavy weather

A sea anchor should be used to prevent a boat from making leeway *only as a last resort.*

Sea anchors produce a tremendous strain on the hull and rigging, and in effect, rob the boat of some of its buoyancy.

When the sea anchor is streamed from the stern, the boat is in danger of being pooped or pitch-poled.

When the sea anchor is streamed from the bow, the boat can easily be thrown backwards and the rudder damaged.

Generally, it is easier to stream and control a sea anchor from the stern. However, boats with narrow hulls, no

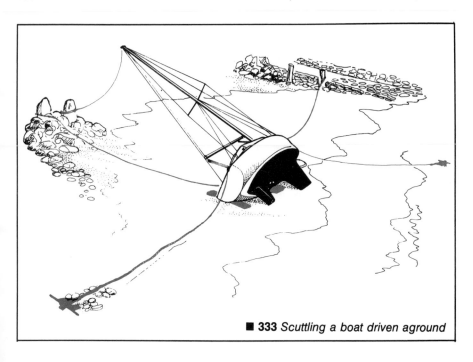

■ **333** *Scuttling a boat driven aground*

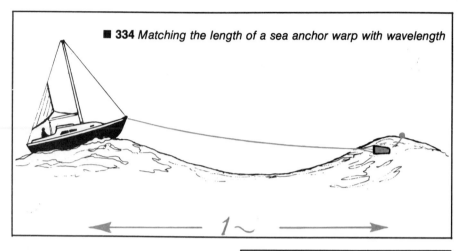

■ 334 *Matching the length of a sea anchor warp with wavelength*

self-draining cockpit and little buoyancy aft should stream a sea anchor from the bow.

Procedure

The warp

As a general rule, the diameter and material of the sea anchor warp should be the same as that of an anchor warp.

The preferable material is nylon due to its elasticity.

If the seas are 'regular', that is, distances between crests are nearly uniform, the length of the warp should be about one wavelength, or some multiple thereof **■ 334.**

The warp is tied to a strong point on either the bow or stern. See: Towing

WARNING:

The warp must be well protected against chafe. **See: Chafe**

Rudder **■ 335**

If streaming the sea anchor from the bow: the rudder becomes vulnerable to the seas. The tiller should be lashed amidships with shock cords or rubber straps, so that if the boat is thrown backwards there is some elasticity in the system.

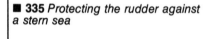

■ 335 *Protecting the rudder against a stern sea*

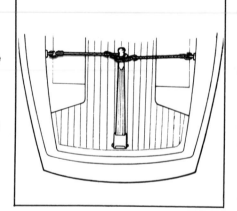

Sails **■ 334**

Traditional, long keel boats will probably lie well under bare poles while streaming a sea anchor.

Modern yachts have a tendency to sheer off. This can be corrected by either:

A jib hanked on the backstay and sheeted amidships.

or

A normal jib sheeted amidships.

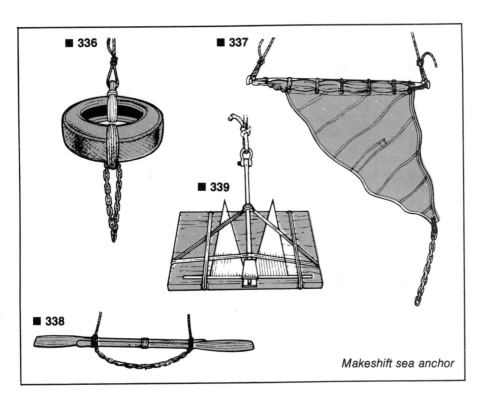

Makeshift sea anchor

A makeshift sea anchor

1 – An old car tyre, with or without a weight ■ **336.**

2 – A sail with or without a spar and weight at its head ■ **337.**

3 – Two oars lashed together and weighted ■ **338.**

4 – A plank securely lashed to a small anchor, and, if necessary, given some flotation from a life-jacket or a lifering ■ **339.**

Sea-cocks

To free a frozen or jammed valve

METHOD 1

Tap it gently with a hammer.

METHOD 2

Heat it with a blow torch, while protecting the surrounding area with wet rags ■ **340.**

METHOD 3

Exert more leverage by lashing a screwdriver, bottlescrew, or piece of pipe or wood to the ring. Be careful not to apply too much pressure and damage the fitting ■ **341.**

A leaky sea-cock

Unscrew the fitting *only* a few turns.

Wrap the threads with oakum, tape, or if necessary, glue or epoxy.

Tighten the fitting.

■ **341** *Freeing a frozen sea-cock*

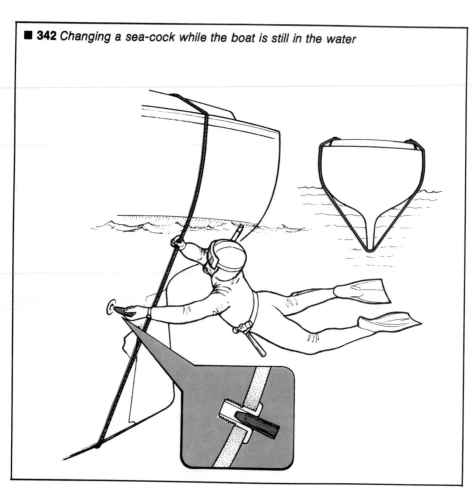

■ **342** *Changing a sea-cock while the boat is still in the water*

To change a sea-cock while the boat is in the water ■ 342

METHOD 1

See: Aground, Careening

METHOD 2

Working under water

Tie a rope under the keel, which can be used as a handhold while working under water.

Cut a piece of soft wood in the shape of a conical plug so that the small end just fits into the hull.

Knock the plug into the fitting from the outside.

Remove and replace the sea-cock from inside the hull.

NOTE:

To fit a new plastic hose on a sea-cock

Place the end in a pot of hot water for a few moments. When it is soft, *immediately* thrust it over the fitting. Secure it with a Jubilee clip.

To repair a leaky hose ■ 343

Use tape,

or

Cut the hose in two, and trim away any worn material. Join the two ends together by placing a piece of smaller hose or pipe inside them. Clamp both ends with wire or Jubilee clips.

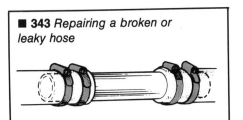

■ **343** *Repairing a broken or leaky hose*

Sea-sickness

Symptoms

Headache.

A cold sweat.

A feeling of weakness and apathy.

Nausea and vomiting.

In extreme cases, depression to the point of suicide.

Treatment

Don't go below. Stay in the fresh air.

Keep warm and dry.

Avoid the sun.

Drink very little.

No alcohol.

Eat small amounts of soft food every few hours.

Close your eyes, or focus only on the horizon.

Medication

NOTE:

Most of the anti-sea-sickness drugs have proven to be effective, but since vomiting is nearly always a problem, those in suppository form are often the most useful.

Tranquillizers appear to have little effect in combating sea-sickness.

	Dosage	
England		
Dramamine	50mg.	
	1–2 hrs. before departure, then 3 times per day	

	Dosage	
France		
Primperan	1 tablet	
	3 times per day	

	Dosage

Germany

Bonamine   25mg.=1 tablet
1–2 tablets 1–2 hrs.
before departure, then 3
times per day

Explanation

The motion of the boat disturbs the normal equilibrium of the inner ear, producing a sensation of instability. This is intensified by the visual perception of movement and the irritation of food rolling in the digestive tract. Another important factor is expectation, the psychological fear of becoming sick, which sometimes creates its own self-fulfilling prophesy.

Nine out of ten people are likely to become sea-sick.

Those most susceptible are:
Women.
Children aged 2–10.
The thin.
The anaemic.
The nervous.
The overweight.

Those nearly immune are:
The old.
The very young.
The deaf.

Prevention

The equilibrium of the inner ear can be trained. A few exercises, done morning and evening, several days before a voyage can be surprisingly helpful.

1 – Stand with your feet wide apart and sway your body in a circular motion for 5–10 minutes.

2 – Practise rolling your eyes in imitation of the boat's movement for several minutes at a time. If this produces a slight nausea, stop until it passes, then continue.

Seiches

Immediately, prepare for a tidal-like change in water level of up to two metres.
See: Aground, Chafe, Drying out, fenders

This change can occur at intervals of from a few minutes up to several hours.

Seiches do *not* forecast a coming storm. Rather, they are the result of the passing of a depression. Generally, they are seasonal – often only in the spring – and localized, for example, the western Spanish coast.

Self-steering

Sheet to tiller gear

Nearly any boat can be made to steer herself, on nearly any course, by a sheet to tiller arrangement. Some experimentation will, of course, be necessary.

Principle

Some part of the running rigging is led to the helm to pull it to windward. This pull should increase when the boat luffs, and slacken when the boat bears away. When the weather helm is more than is necessary, it can be balanced by an elastic.

The sheet should pull to windward.

The elastic should pull to leeward.

The elastic should be slack when the rudder is amidships.

NOTE:

Any sail or course change will require an adjustment of the system, and this may entail shifting from one method to another.

To windward

Elastic or rubber tubing supplies weather
helm ■ **344, 345.**

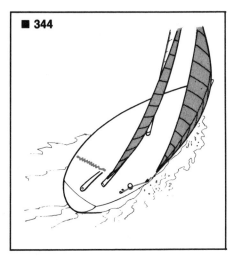

■ 344

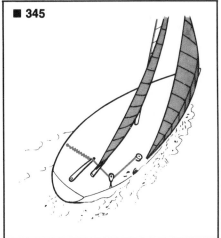

■ 345

On a broad reach

Foresail control ■ **346, 347.**

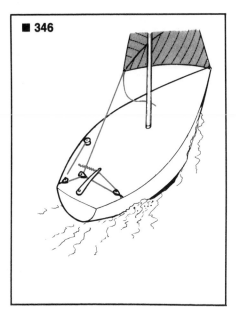

■ 346

■ 347

In light winds

Main boom control.

■ 348

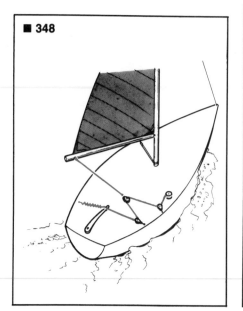

■ 350 *Using a jib as a make-shift windvane*

■ 349 Running

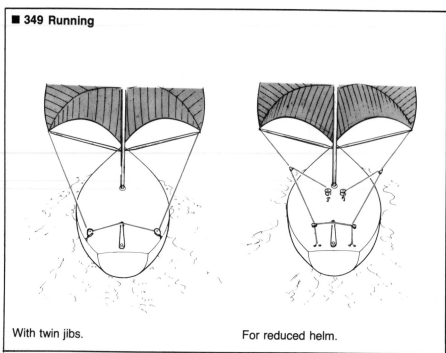

With twin jibs.

For reduced helm.

When the wind is abaft the beam

A small jib can be hanked on the backstay.

A spar or oar is tied along the foot of the sail and one end lashed or shackled to the backstay.

Lines tied to the clew are run through blocks on either side of the cockpit and then to the tiller.

WARNING:

Should the boat gybe the sail will foul the main boom.

Semaphore

Sextant

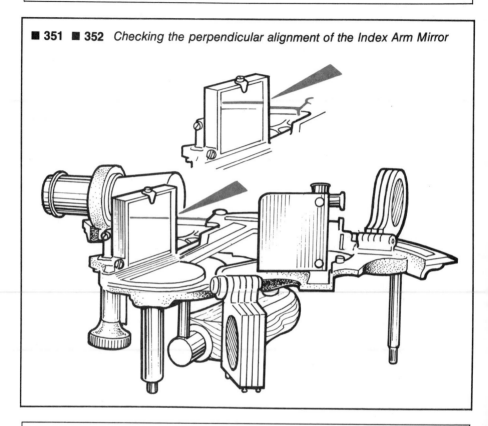

■ 351 ■ 352 *Checking the perpendicular alignment of the Index Arm Mirror*

Mirror adjustment

Principle

The two mirrors, the Index Arm Mirror and the Horizon Mirror, must be correctly aligned for an accurate reflection of the sun.

The centre of the face of the Horizon Mirror must be at 45 degrees to a base line running from the centre of the eyepiece to the centre of the mirror.

The centre of the Index Arm Mirror must be directly over the point of pivot, and the face of the mirror along a line from the pivot to the zero point on the scale.

Both mirrors must be at an angle of 90 degrees to the face of the sextant.

Procedure

To check the perpendicular alignment of the Index Arm Mirror ■ 351, 352

Hold the sextant flat side up.

Set the Index Arm at about 35 degrees.

Look at the Index Arm Mirror. If the arc reflected in the mirror, and the arc behind it are a continuous line, then the mirror is perpendicular.

If there is a break in the line, then the mirror must be adjusted by the screws on the reverse side.

To check the perpendicular aligment of the Horizon Mirror ■ 353

Hold the sextant in the normal fashion.

Set the Index Arm at zero.

Sight the horizon, and adjust the micrometer so that the half in the clear side and the half on the silvered side meet.

Turn the sextant to about 45 degrees.

If the horizon line does *not* break, the mirror is in adjustment.

If the line separates, the mirror should be adjusted by the screws on the reverse side.

Index Error are plus or minus 8′. Past that point the mirrors should be adjusted.

Procedure

Set the Index Arm at exactly zero.

Sight the horizon.

Adjust the arm until the two halves of the horizon meet – the half reflected from the Index Mirror and the one sighted through the clear portion of the Horizon Mirror ■ 354.

Record the angle:
If it is negative – below the zero mark – the Index Error must be added.
If it is positive – above the zero mark – the Index Error must be subtracted.

■ 353 *Checking the perpendicular alignment of the Horizon Mirror*

■ 354 *Finding the Index Error*

Index Error

Principle

The two sextant mirrors need *not* be in perfect vertical alignment to each other. A small error can be tolerated and most sextants have one. However, it must be known and included in the calculation of a sight. The generally accepted limits for

Cleaning

Should the sextant become immersed in salt water or coated with spray, it should be carefully rinsed and cleaned with fresh water, dried and the joints oiled with a light machine oil.

Longitude without a sextant – Meridian Passage by Horizon Sight

Prerequisites

A clear sunrise followed by a clear sunset.

GMT

The Date.
If this is not known, an approximation to within two days will cause a possible error of 15′ of longitude, no more than 15 nautical miles.

The Nautical Almanac

Principle

Longitude is nearly synonymous with Time as both are used to measure the eastward or westward distance from the Greenwich meridian. 360° Longitude, or the distance around the world, equals 24 hours. 180° equals 12 hours, and one degree equals four minutes. **See: Time** for an Arc (Longitude) to Time conversion table.

Therefore, if you know the precise instant the sun crosses your meridian – that is, passes directly overhead – by simple subtraction you can find the difference (in Time) between your Meridian Passage and the one at Greenwich which is listed in *The Nautical Almanac*. That figure, in Time (hours and minutes), can be converted easily into Arc (degrees and minutes) and so become Longitude.

Procedure

Record in GMT the exact moment of sunrise: when the sun's lower limb touches the horizon.

On the same day record the moment of sunset, again when the sun's lower limb touches the horizon.

Compute the elapsed time between sunrise and sunset, then divide it by two.

That figure, in hours and minutes, when added to the moment of sunrise is the

instant the sun was directly overhead – it's Meridian Passage.

In *The Nautical Almanac*, under the correct date, in the lower right-hand corner of the right-hand page is the time of Meridian Passage at Greenwich.

Compute the difference – in Time – between your moment of Meridian Passage and the one at Greenwich.

Convert that Time (hours and minutes) into Arc (degrees and minutes) which is Longitude.

See: Time – Table for the Conversion of Arc (Longitude) to Time (p.230).

A Sun sight without a sextant

Prerequisites

A clear sunrise or sunset.

The Date.

GMT

The Nautical Almanac

Sight Reduction Tables – but *not* HO 214 (HD 486) which does not tabulate below five° of Altitude.

Principle

Theoretically, a Sun sight can be taken at any time during the day when it can be observed clearly. Twice during the day it is possible to know the sun's position in the sky without the aid of a sextant.

At sunrise and sunset, even with the naked eye, one can record the instant the lower limb touches the horizon. The 'observed altitude' becomes 0°, and the sight can then be worked out in the normal fashion. A horizon sight will not be as accurate as one taken above 10° and will require additional corrections, none the less, if carefully observed and calculated, it can provide a reliable position line.

Procedure

Using either the naked eye or a pair of

$$\frac{\text{Time between sunrise \& sunset}}{2} + \begin{array}{c}\text{GMT of}\\ \text{sunrise}\end{array} = \begin{array}{c}\text{GMT of your}\\ \text{Meridian Passage}\end{array}$$

$$\begin{array}{c}\text{GMT of Meridian}\\ \text{Passage at Greenwich}\end{array} - \begin{array}{c}\text{GMT of your}\\ \text{Meridian Passage}\end{array} = \begin{array}{c}\text{Distance in}\\ \text{Time to Greenwich}\end{array}$$

Convert: The Time Distance to Greenwich into longitude degrees and minutes using the Arc to Time Table

binoculars, watch the sun until its lower limb touches the horizon.

WARNING:

Use a protective shade. If one is not available, a piece of glass held over a candle for a few moments or a dark strip of photographic film will make a good substitute.

Record the time for the passage of both the upper and lower limbs. Although only one is necessary, two sights always provide a partial check.

Compute the sight in the normal fashion using Sight Reduction Tables, *except:*

1 – When correcting – subtracing – for refraction, use an Apparent Altitude of 0°.
For the sun, this is:
Upper limb −50.3′
Lower limb −18.3′
For stars and planets −34.5′

2 – Additional corrections must be made for temperature and barometric pressure. **See: Time** for a *Table for Barometric and Temperature Corrections of a Horizon Sight* (p.000).

Your course without a sextant

Prerequisites

A clear night.

The Date – an approximation is sufficient.

The Nautical Almanac.

GMT

An accurate compass.

A Star Finder – The one in *The Nautical Almanac* will suffice.

Principle

Every heavenly body has its 'ground point', or Geographic Position, the point on earth which is directly beneath it. Obviously, this changes from moment to moment, but if you can find a star which will pass directly over your destination and know precisely at what time this will occur, then a bearing from you to the star at that instant will be your course. It is often called 'The Star of Bethlehem principle'.

The celestial coordinates are analogous to those of the earth. Instead of Latitude a star is given a Declination, and for 57

Horizon Sight

Observed Altitude Zero degrees Lower limb	− The Dip	− 18.3′	± Corrections for Temperature & Barometric Pressure	= True Altitude

stars these Declinations are listed on the left pages of *The Nautical Almanac* under the heading 'Stars – Dec'.

If you select a star whose declination is roughly the same as the Latitude of your destination, then at some point in time that star must have its 'ground point' at or near to that of your destination.

When this occurs is dependent on its Longitude, which is computed from its Sidereal Hour Angle (listed in the column under 'S.H.A.') *plus* the Greenwich Hour Angle of Aries – which is given on the left side of the page. At the moment these two figures total your Longitude, the star is directly above your destination.

Procedure

For the appropriate date in *The Nautical Almanac*, read down the list of stars under the column 'Stars – Dec' until you find a star with approximately the same declination as the latitude of your destination.

Record the Sidereal Hour Angle listed in the adjacent column, then *subtract* it from the longitude of your destination.

If the longitude of your destination is smaller than the Sidereal Hour Angle of the star, *add* 360 to your Longitude.

If the longitude of your destination is an easterly one, *subtract* it first from 360.

The result is the G.H.A. – Greenwich Hour Angle – of Aries. Match that position with the time – shown in G.M.T. – in the adjacent column, and at that moment the star is above your destination.

Locate the star with a Star Finder or the star charts in *The Nautical Almanac*. **See: Stars**

At the proper moment, sight the star over an accurate compass.

The bearing is your course.

A makeshift sextant

Materials

One piece of plywood or hardboard.

Two pieces of mirror – approximately 2×3cm. each with a minimum of one straight edge.

Two wooden blocks – approximately 2×3cm.

Two or three 5cm. strips of darkened photographic film, preferably the leader of a developed roll, or strips of dark plastic bag.

One empty 35mm. film container, or an equal sized plastic bottle.

One drawer handle.

Five screws.

20cm. dark coloured thread.

Procedure

Cut out the scale on the opposite page and glue it to the plywood.

Drill the hole for the Index Arm pivot ■ **358.**

Using the template, cut the Index Arm from another piece of wood.

Drill a hole in the centre of each of the two blocks, and glue a mirror to one side. These will become the Index and Horizon Mirrors.

Drill a small hole – pencil lead size – in

| Your Longitude | – | SHA | A Star whose Declination | = | Latitude of your Destination | = | GHA of Aries |

When Aries has that GHA a bearing to the star = Your Course.

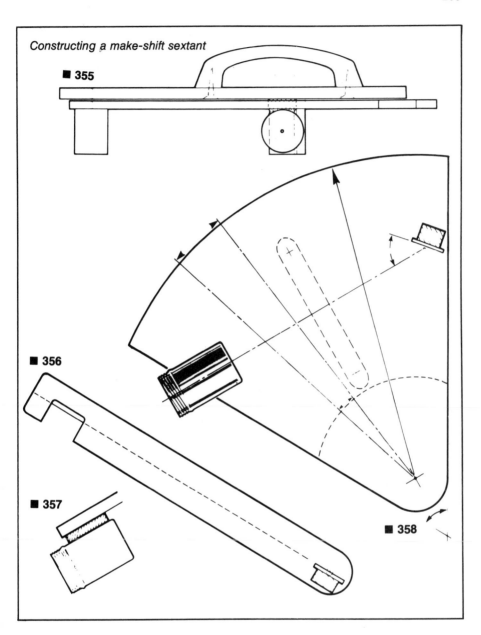

Constructing a make-shift sextant

■ 355

■ 356

■ 357

■ 358

the centre of the film container bottom, then glue it in place with its horizontal axis along the line ■ 355.

Mount the Horizon Mirror ■ 356 with its *face* along the *45 degree angle* and its axis at point ■ 357.

Mount the Index Mirror with its *face* over the *centre* of the Index Arm pivot ■ 358.

Attach the Index Arm with a large screw, and tie one end of the thread around the screw. Glue or tie the other end to the lower tip of the Index Arm so that the thread passes the zero point on the compass rose and the zero point on the scale.

Mount the handle on the back.

Bend the film into slides or cut the plastic into strips and put as many as necessary over the mirrors. Tie in place with rubber bands or string.

Adjust the Index Error by slightly changing the position of the thread.

NOTE:

The hole on the Index Mirror block should be slightly larger than the screw to allow for Index Error adjustment when the sextant is completed.

Each mirror must be mounted at exactly 90 degrees to the surface of the sextant.

Sharks

If someone is in the water

A number of researchers report that noise will frighten sharks away:

1 – Start the engine.
2 – Beat on the hull.
3 – Fire a rifle into the water.

For the swimmer

Shout into the water.

Beat on diving tanks.

If spear fishing, release any catch.

Face the shark and swim slowly back to the boat.

WARNING:

Do not urinate if a shark is nearby. When a shark attacks, he first dives then turns on his back. This means that as long as you can see the dorsal fin you are safe.

NOTE:

Wearing clothing in the water appears to offer some protection in that sharks are *more likely* to be attracted to a naked swimmer than a fully dressed one.

If attacked

'Quiet aggression' is the best tactic.

Sharks will generally test their prey (hitting it with their nose or body) before striking. When they do, they should be struck forcefully with either hands or feet.

A hasty retreat can be very dangerous, as it is senseless to try to outswim a shark.

Shoals and sandbars

See also: Aground, drying out

When wind and tide are in the same direction

A smooth slick will probably indicate deeper water.

When wind and tide are in contrary directions

Rough wavelets will probably indicate deeper water.

If caught on shoals

Do *not* try to ride the backs of waves.

If under power:

Accelerate when the stern falls towards a wave's overhang.

Throttle back when the bows fall away.

WARNING:

Never tow a dinghy over a bar. It could easily fill with water, sink, and act as a powerful sea anchor.

Sharks that are known to be dangerous

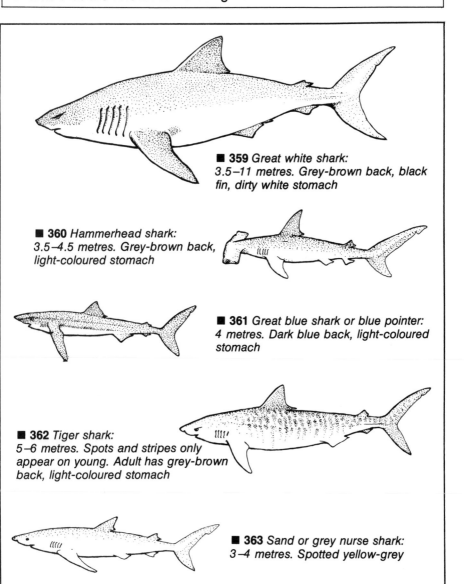

■ **359** *Great white shark:
3.5–11 metres. Grey-brown back, black
fin, dirty white stomach*

■ **360** *Hammerhead shark:
3.5–4.5 metres. Grey-brown back,
light-coloured stomach*

■ **361** *Great blue shark or blue pointer:
4 metres. Dark blue back, light-coloured
stomach*

■ **362** *Tiger shark:
5–6 metres. Spots and stripes only
appear on young. Adult has grey-brown
back, light-coloured stomach*

■ **363** *Sand or grey nurse shark:
3–4 metres. Spotted yellow-grey*

■ **364** *Mako:
5 metres. Shiny silver sides,
blue back, white stomach*

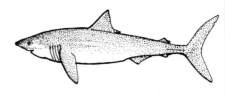

Shock

Symptoms

Can accompany any serious injury or illness, sea-sickness included.

Person becomes cold, pale, sweaty and extremely weak.

Fainting will probaly occur.

Treatment

Immediate rest, with the feet slightly elevated above the head.

Warmth.

If the person is conscious

A hot drink – but *no alcohol.*

If the person is unconscious and not breathing

Begin immediately mouth-to-mouth resuscitation.

See: Artificial respiration

Shrouds

See: Rigging Failures

Sight Reduction Tables

Finding longitude without Sight Reduction Tables

Prerequisites

A sextant.

The Nautical Almanac.

GMT

The Date.

Principle

Longitude and time are virtually synonymous – 360° of longitude equals 24 hours, one degree equals four minutes. Therefore, if one is known, the other can be calculated quickly. **See: Time** – Conversion of Arc (longitude) to Time.

If one can determine the precise moment, in hours, minutes and seconds, when the sun passes directly overhead, that is, the instant of Meridian Passage, then the difference between that Meridian Passage and the one at Greenwich, which is given in *The Nautical Almanac*, can easily be found by addition or subtraction. This difference in Time can then be converted into longitude and marked off from the Greenwich Meridian.

The complication is that of knowing exactly when the sun is directly overhead, since the sun often remains several minutes at its apex. However, one can choose a Time earlier and later in the day when the sun's movement is more rapid. By carefully measuring the elapsed time between two points, one in the morning and the other in the afternoon, when the sun's elevation above the horizon is the same, and dividing by two, Meridian Passage can be accurately determined.

Procedure

Take a morning sun sight 2–4 hours before the approximate time of Meridian Passage and carefully note the sextant reading and the GMT in hours, minutes and seconds.

After Meridian Passage, in the afternoon, follow the sun on its downwards arc until it reaches the precise angle of your morning sight. Again carefully note the time in hours, minutes and seconds.

Calculate the elapsed time between the two sights.

Divide it by two.

Add the result to the time of your morning sight.

The answer is the time of Meridian Passage, that is, the moment the sun crossed your meridian. Next, find the time

$$\frac{\text{GMT of afternoon sight} - \text{GMT of morning sight (same elevation)}}{2} + \text{GMT of morning sight} = \text{GMT of your Meridian Passage}$$

$$\text{GMT of Meridian Passage at Greenwich} - \text{GMT of your Meridian Passage} = \text{Distance in Time to Greenwich}$$

Convert: The Time distance to Greenwich into longitude degrees and minutes using the Arc to Time Table.

of Meridian Passage at Greenwich. This is given in *The Nautical Almanac*, under the appropriate date, on the right-hand pages, in the lower right-hand corner under the heading 'Sun – Mer. Pass'.

Calculate the difference in Time between your Meridian Passage and the one at Greenwich. Convert that Time difference into longitude **See: Time** – Conversion of Arc (longitude) to Time. The result is your longitude, to be marked off east or west, depending upon your position relative to the Greenwich Meridian.

Finding latitude without Sight Reduction Tables

Prerequisites

A sextant.

The Date.

The Nautical Almanac.

Approximate time in GMT

Principle

At local noon, your noon, when the sun is directly overhead, a position line drawn at right angles to the sun's bearing would be along an east-west axis, that is, on a latitude. Twice during the year – at solstice – the sun's angle at that moment would equal latitude. At other times one must add or subtract the sun's Declination, that is, its 'latitude in the heavens'.

Procedure

Sight the sun in the late morning, and follow it as it rises. Record its highest altitude.

Find the right-hand page in *The Nautical Almanac* for the appropriate date. (These pages list the sun's Declination in degrees and minutes for every hour of the year under the heading – 'Sun – Dec.') Using the time to the nearest hour – in GMT – record the sun's Declination, its direction – north or south indicated by N or S – and angle in degrees and minutes.

If the direction and your hemisphere are the *same, add* the Declination to the sun's Altitude to find your latitude.

If the direction and your hemisphere are *different* (contrary, that is, one north, the other, south), *subtract* the declination from the sun's Altitude to find your latitude.

$$\text{Altitude of the Sun at Meridian Passage} \pm \text{Sun's Declination at that time in GMT} = \text{Your Latitude}$$

NOTE:

The sun often appears to 'sit' at its apex for a few moments before beginning its descent.

Signal mirror

See: Heliograph

Sleeping pills

	Weak Dosage
England	
Valium	10mg.
Equanil	400mg.

	Strong Dosage
Mogadon	1–2 5mg. tablets
Amylobarbitone	1–2 100mg. tablets

	Weak Dosage
France	
Valium	10mg.
Equanil	400mg.

	Strong Dosage
Mogadan	1–2 5mg. tablets
Immenoctal	1–2 100mg. tablets

	Weak Dosage
Germany	
Valium	10mg.
Revonal Retard	300mg.

	Strong Dosage
Mogadan	1–2 5mg. tablets
Nembutal	1–2 100mg. tablets

NOTE:

If a person has sustained a serious injury at sea, it is easier on the crew and the injured man if he is kept under sedation until arrival in port.

WARNING:

Do not administer these drugs more than four times a day.

Solar still

See also: Distillation, Water

Materials ■ 365

A large, wide-mouthed pot or tin.

A few rags.

A glass or bowl.

A sheet of plastic, preferably dark in colour.

■ 365 *A makeshift solar still*

Procedure

Place the glass in the centre of the pot and lay the rags around it.

Fill the pot $\frac{1}{4}$ to $\frac{1}{3}$ full with salt water.

Tie the plastic sheet over the pot and put a weight, such as a stone or shackle, in the middle of it.

Put the pot in the sun.

Principle

The sun's heat will cause the water to evaporate and condense on the plastic sheet where it will run down to the centre and drip into the glass.

Sound signals

See: Fog

Spanish reef

An emergency reef to replace a small foresail or ease the strain on a damaged head:

An ordinary overhand knot at the head will make a small reduction.

A larger reduction should be made with a figure eight knot.

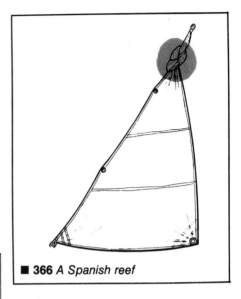

■ **366** *A Spanish reef*

NOTE:

Canvas sails may be stretched and damaged in this manner. Modern Terylene sails are hardly affected, but the wire may be damaged in the knot.

Spanish windlass

Purpose ■ **367**

Whenever more leverage is required and a winch is either broken or unavailable.

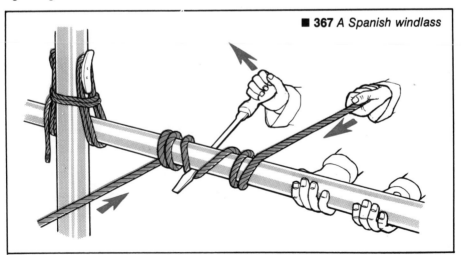

■ **367** *A Spanish windlass*

Procedure

A spar, preferably one of sizeable diameter, is lodged against the mast. A loose lashing may be necessary to prevent it from sliding off.

One person holds the outer end, while a second winds the line around the spar, taking a turn at a time with a large screwdriver or lever of some kind.

Speedometer

See: Log

Sprains

Treatment

Limit the activity of the limb.

Elevate it to reduce swelling and pain.

Apply cold salt water compresses for the first 24 hours, then hot ones.

If necessary, bind the joint for support. When binding a sprain always begin at the furthest point on the extremity and bind towards the body.

Stars

The North, or Pole, Star ■ 368

A line drawn from Merak to Dubhe, the two outer stars of the Plough (Big Dipper, or Great Bear), and extended *five times* will reach the North Star.

NOTE:

When looking for the Plough, remember that it occupies about 40° in the sky.

See: Distance-off – natural hand angles (p.65)

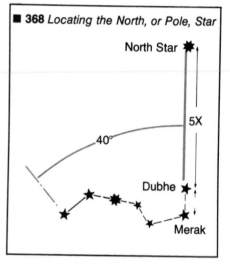

■ **368** *Locating the North, or Pole, Star*

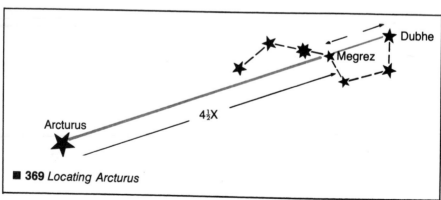

■ **369** *Locating Arcturus*

Locating other navigational stars from the Plough

Arcturus ■ 369

A line drawn from Dubhe to Megrez and extended $4\frac{1}{2}$ *times* will reach Arcturus.

Vega ■ 370

Draw a line from Alkaid, the last star on the Plough's handle to the North Star. Another line taken from its mid-point and drawn perpendicular, $1\frac{1}{3}$ *times* as long as the first line will reach Vega.

Altair ■ 371

Complete the triangle used to find Vega by drawing a hypotenuse from Alkaid to Vega. Extend that line by $\frac{2}{3}$ and it will reach Altair.

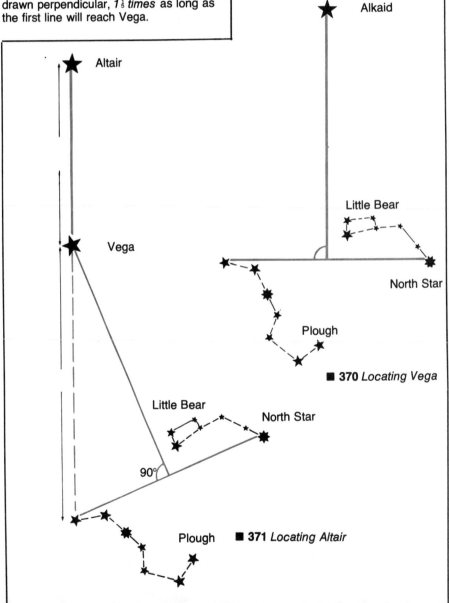

■ **370** *Locating Vega*

■ **371** *Locating Altair*

Capella ■ 372

Draw a line across the Plough's two pointers – Merak and Dubhe – to the North Star. Draw a second line perpendicular to it, extend it until it is $1\frac{1}{3}$ the distance from Dubhe to the North Star and it will reach Capella.

Deneb ■ 373

Draw a line from Phecda to Megrez, the two inner stars of the Plough, and extend it to the tip of the Little Bear. Double the distance and it will reach Deneb.

Steel hull repair

Leaks

A small crack or hole can be filled with mastic, filler, cold solder, glass fibre or epoxy resin.

Holes

METHOD 1   A riveted steel or metal patch

See: Aluminium repair

METHOD 2   A glass fibre patch

See: Glass fibre repair

Sterilization

See also: Antiseptics

In emergency conditions, it is impossible to sterilize an implement such as a knife or a sewing needle fully. However, partial sterilization can be achieved by:

Boiling the object for at least 20 minutes.

Heating it over a flame for two minutes.

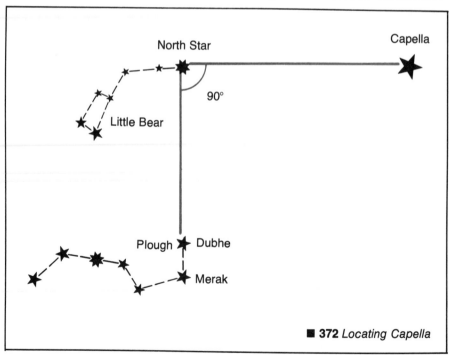

■ **372** *Locating Capella*

Soaking it in a solution of one cup bleach and one litre water.

Soaking it in alcohol – at least a 70% solution.

NOTE:

After the implement is sterilized be sure that only other sterilized materials come in contact with it.

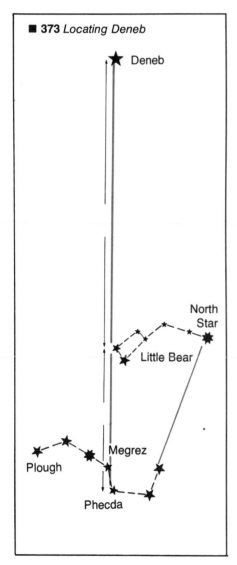

■ 373 *Locating Deneb*

Deneb

North Star

Little Bear

Plough

Megrez

Phecda

Stop

International Code of Signals

'L'

LIMA

'YOU SHOULD STOP YOUR VESSEL INSTANTLY.'

Yellow   Black

■ 374

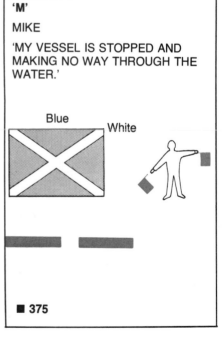

'M'

MIKE

'MY VESSEL IS STOPPED AND MAKING NO WAY THROUGH THE WATER.'

Blue   White

■ 375

Storm warning signals

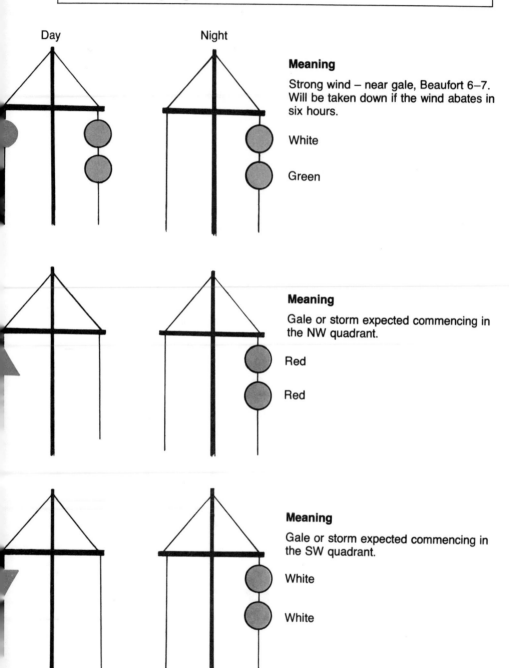

Day   Night

Meaning

Strong wind – near gale, Beaufort 6–7.
Will be taken down if the wind abates in
six hours.

White

Green

Meaning

Gale or storm expected commencing in
the NW quadrant.

Red

Red

Meaning

Gale or storm expected commencing in
the SW quadrant.

White

White

International system of visual storm warning signals

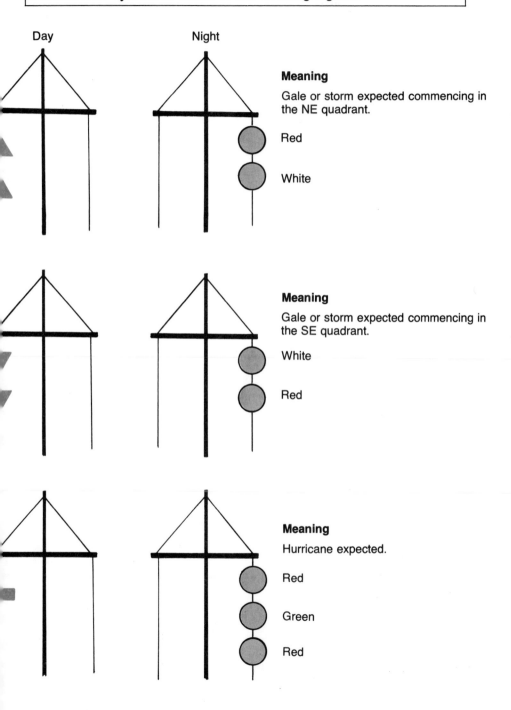

Day   Night

Meaning

Gale or storm expected commencing in the NE quadrant.

Red

White

Meaning

Gale or storm expected commencing in the SE quadrant.

White

Red

Meaning

Hurricane expected.

Red

Green

Red

During daytime *flags* may be shown

One flag – white or red: Wind expected to veer.

Two flags – white or red: Wind expected to back.

NOTE:

Many countries have national or local visual storm warning signals which are displayed in conjunction with the international ones. These signals are described in the appropriate volumes of the sailing directions.

English system of visual storm warnings

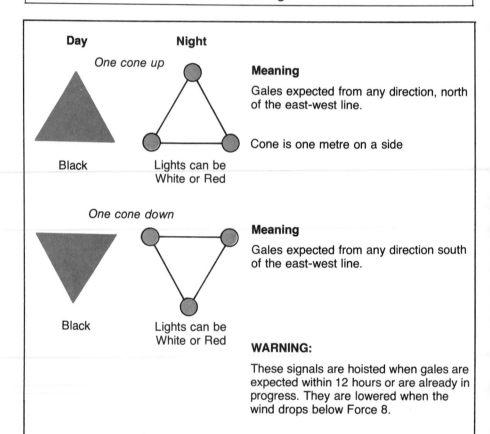

Day   **Night**

One cone up

Black   Lights can be White or Red

Meaning

Gales expected from any direction, north of the east-west line.

Cone is one metre on a side

One cone down

Black   Lights can be White or Red

Meaning

Gales expected from any direction south of the east-west line.

WARNING:

These signals are hoisted when gales are expected within 12 hours or are already in progress. They are lowered when the wind drops below Force 8.

Stormsails

Trysail ■ 376

The sail area should be smaller than a reefed-down mainsail. It can be hoisted on all points of sailing.

Rigging a trysail

Lash the boom amidships.

Take down the mainsail.

Hoist the trysail on the main halyard.

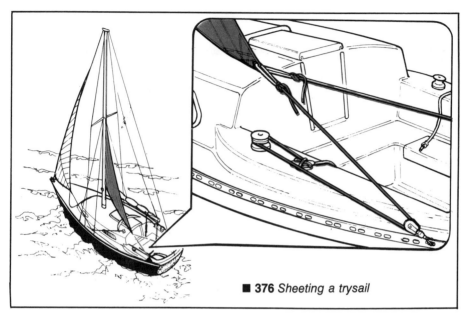

■ **376** *Sheeting a trysail*

Sheeting a Trysail

METHOD 1

If the boom is short, the trysail can be sheeted like a jib, with a sheet to each side run through a block well aft. This method of sheeting is preferable when there is a danger of gybing.

METHOD 2

The trysail is sheeted to the end of the boom and can be trimmed by the

mainsheet. This method of sheeting makes it easier to tack.

A makeshift trysail

A jib as a trysail

METHOD 1 ■ 377, 378, 379

The sail foot is placed against the mast. To fit properly, the foot must be reinforced, either by sewing hooks to the bolt rope which can be clipped to the sail slides, or by cutting eyelets and passing lines around the mast secured by toggles.

■ **377** *The jib as a trysail*

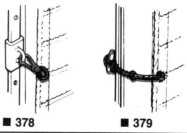

■ **378**   ■ **379**

METHOD 2 ■ 380

Lash the tack around the gooseneck ■ **380A.**

Pass a bight of line through the head and around the mast ■ **380B.**

Tighten the luff with a halyard winch.

Sheet the clew to the end of the boom ■ **380C.**

If the leech is slack, bowse the sheet down at the proper angle to the boom. Use the mainsheet to control the boom ■ **380D.**

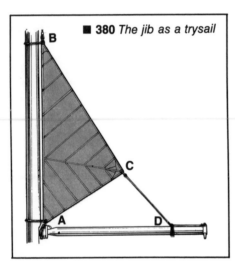

■ **380** *The jib as a trysail*

Jibs

As a general rule, a working jib takes up approximately 75% of the fore-triangle. A storm jib should take up only about 40%. Its luff should not overlap the mast. Its foot should be cut high, so that it won't be vulnerable to oncoming waves.

A makeshift storm jib ■ 381

The Dacron (Terylene) material of a storm sail is the same as that of a set of working sails. Hence, to serve as a storm jib, a normal jib need only be reefed. A set of points and eyelets can be sewn in and cringles positioned for a new tack and clew.

Streaming a warp

See: Running

Submarines

On normal exercises, when surfacing

Two yellow flares are released to the surface at intervals of three minutes.

In emergency

A series of red flares is released to the surface.

Sunburn

See also: Burns, Heat exhaustion, Sunstroke

Treatment

If severe
Treat as a burn. **See: Burns**

■ **381** *A makeshift storm jib*

If accompanied by chills, fever and/or swelling:

Apply cool compresses of:

Three tablespoons vinegar and one litre fresh water

or

Three tablespoons baking soda (Sodium bicarbonate) and one litre fresh water

or

One tablespoon Epsom salts (Magnesium sulphate) and one litre fresh water.

Drink plenty of fluids – at least one litre every three hours.

Take Vitamin C – 1gm. per hour for the first six hours.

NOTE:

If suntan lotion is not available, olive oil, coconut oil, or simply cooking oil mixed with a few drops of Iodine can be used to screen the sun's rays.

Sunstroke

See also: Heat exhaustion

Symptoms

Usually occurs after vigorous exercise.

Skin is dry, flushed and hot.

Confusion.

Dizziness.

Loss of consciousness.

NOTE:

By contrast, in a condition of *Heat exhaustion*, the skin is pale and moist.

Treatment

Immediately lower the victim's body temperature

Place him in the shade and fan him.

Put him in a tub of cool water.

Sponge or throw water on him.

NOTE:

Sunstroke is essentially a total collapse of the body's heat regulation system. Without immediate treatment, body temperature will continue to rise and cause either death or brain damage.

Massage the skin to stimulate circulation.

When conscious, the victim should immediately drink cool liquids.

Recovery will be slow and require at least 48 hours.

T

Tackle

See: Block and tackle

Temperature

See: Weather forecast

Tiller

If the tiller fitting is damaged or broken

Lash a boat-hook or oars to either side
■ **382.**

or

Steer the boat without a tiller ■ **383.**

Drill a hole in the rudder blade near the waterline. Pass lines through the hole, knot them in place then run them back to the cockpit.

or

Screw, bolt or nail a fitting of any kind to the rudder blade near the waterline. Connect two lines and run them back through blocks to the cockpit winches.

To lash a tiller ■ 384

Only one end should be securely lashed down. The other end must be instantly releasable.

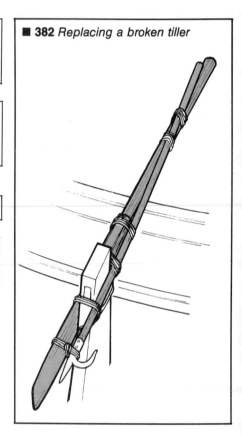

■ **382** *Replacing a broken tiller*

To repair a broken tiller

Break a boat-hook in half and thrust the ends into the fitting.

Or use an oar, or piece of a jib boom.

This can be reinforced by lashing to it:

A large screwdriver.

Bolts, pipe or a bottle screw.

Pieces of floorboard.

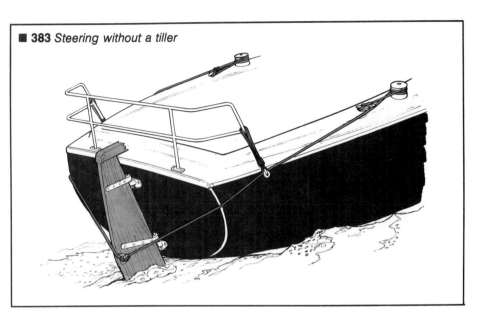

■ **383** *Steering without a tiller*

■ **384** *Lashing down the tiller with a quick release*

Time

Stations that transmit time signals:

Place	Call-Sign	Frequencies (MHz)
Buenos Aires (Argentina)	LOL	5, 10, 15
Shanghai (China)	BPV	5, 10, 15
Liblice (Czechoslovakia)	OMA	2.5
Chevannes (France)	FFH	2.5
Kihei (Hawaii)	WWVH	2.5, 5, 10, 15
New Delhi (India)	ATA	10
Turin Rome (Italy)	IBF IAM	5 5
Tokyo (Japan)	JJY	2.5, 5, 10, 15
Johannesburg (South Africa)	ZUO	10
Rugby (U.K.)	MSF	2.5, 5, 10
Ft. Collins, Colorado (U.S.A.)	WWV	2.5, 5, 10, 15, 20, 25
Moscow (U.S.S.R.)	RWM	2.5, 5, 10, 15

To find GMT by a sunrise or sunset sight

Principle

Latitude can easily be found without an accurate knowledge of Time. **See: Sight reduction tables** – *Latitude by 'Noon Sight'* (p.213).

In computing a normal sight, an error of one minute in time can affect your longitude by as much as 15 minutes, but it will hardly change a position line which runs east-west, that is, longitudinally. If latitude is known and remains constant, any error will be in terms of longitude, which can easily be converted to Time. **See:** *Table for Conversion of Arc (Longitude) to Time* (p.230).

Prerequisites

A clear sunrise or sunset.

Date.

An estimate of G.M.T.

The Nautical Almanac.

Sight Reduction Tables – but not HO 214 (HD 486) which does not tabulate below five degrees of altitude.

Your latitude.

Procedure

Using either the naked eye or a pair of binoculars, watch the sun until the lower limb touches the horizon.

Record the time of passage with your best estimation of G.M.T.

Compute the sight in the normal fashion, *except*:

Correct for an Apparent Altitude of 0 degrees:
Upper Limb −50.3′
Lower Limb −18.3′

Correct for temperature and Barometric pressure. **See:** *Table for Barometric and Temperature Corrections of a Horizon Sight* (p.229).

Plot the position line.

Measure the latitudinal distance – that is, on a north-south line from your Assumed Position to your Position Line.

Convert that distance from degrees and minutes into Time – minutes and seconds by the *Conversion of Arc (Longitude) to Time Table.*

That is the chronometric error.

If your true position is *eastwards* of your Assumed position, the watch is *fast; if westwards, slow.*

WARNING:

Use of protective filter of some kind. If one is not available, a piece of smoked glass or photographic film will make a good substitute.

Toothaches

Treatment

Take something for pain. **See: Pain-killers**

Tap the teeth with the end of a teaspoon to determine exactly which tooth is causing the pain.

If the tooth is sensitive to heat and cold

If the tooth has a hole, try to prise out any remaining bits of filling with a sterilized nail or needle.

Clean the hole and dry it carefully.

Close the hole with a bit of candle wax, or well-chewed gum, or powdered Aspirin. Do not fill the hole, or apply pressure, but, if necessary, a make-shift cap can be made from a layer of cotton wool and epoxy.

If the tooth is not sensitive to heat and cold

More than likely, there is an infection in the gums. This can be checked by feeling for a sore spot.

Take antibiotics. **See: Antibiotics**

If antibiotics are not available, or the infection persists, any remaining bits of filling should be removed and the tooth left open so that the infection can drain through it.

Gargle with camomile or sage tea several times a day.

NOTE:

A tooth, loose from a blow, should be straightened and left in the mouth as quite likely it will renew itself.

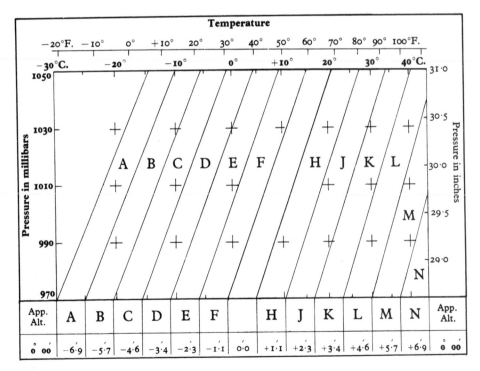

Table for barometric and temperature corrections of a horizon sight

°	0°–59° h m	°	60°–119° h m	°	120°–179° h m	°	180°–239° h m	°	240°–299° h m	°	300°–359° h m	′	0′·00 m s	0′·25 m s	0′·50 m s	0′·75 m s
0	0 00	60	4 00	120	8 00	180	12 00	240	16 00	300	20 00	0	0 00	0 01	0 02	0 03
1	0 04	61	4 04	121	8 04	181	12 04	241	16 04	301	20 04	1	0 04	0 05	0 06	0 07
2	0 08	62	4 08	122	8 08	182	12 08	242	16 08	302	20 08	2	0 08	0 09	0 10	0 11
3	0 12	63	4 12	123	8 12	183	12 12	243	16 12	303	20 12	3	0 12	0 13	0 14	0 15
4	0 16	64	4 16	124	8 16	184	12 16	244	16 16	304	20 16	4	0 16	0 17	0 18	0 19
5	0 20	65	4 20	125	8 20	185	12 20	245	16 20	305	20 20	5	0 20	0 21	0 22	0 23
6	0 24	66	4 24	126	8 24	186	12 24	246	16 24	306	20 24	6	0 24	0 25	0 26	0 27
7	0 28	67	4 28	127	8 28	187	12 28	247	16 28	307	20 28	7	0 28	0 29	0 30	0 31
8	0 32	68	4 32	128	8 32	188	12 32	248	16 32	308	20 32	8	0 32	0 33	0 34	0 35
9	0 36	69	4 36	129	8 36	189	12 36	249	16 36	309	20 36	9	0 36	0 37	0 38	0 39
10	0 40	70	4 40	130	8 40	190	12 40	250	16 40	310	20 40	10	0 40	0 41	0 42	0 43
11	0 44	71	4 44	131	8 44	191	12 44	251	16 44	311	20 44	11	0 44	0 45	0 46	0 47
12	0 48	72	4 48	132	8 48	192	12 48	252	16 48	312	20 48	12	0 48	0 49	0 50	0 51
13	0 52	73	4 52	133	8 52	193	12 52	253	16 52	313	20 52	13	0 52	0 53	0 54	0 55
14	0 56	74	4 56	134	8 56	194	12 56	254	16 56	314	20 56	14	0 56	0 57	0 58	0 59
15	1 00	75	5 00	135	9 00	195	13 00	255	17 00	315	21 00	15	1 00	1 01	1 02	1 03
16	1 04	76	5 04	136	9 04	196	13 04	256	17 04	316	21 04	16	1 04	1 05	1 06	1 07
17	1 08	77	5 08	137	9 08	197	13 08	257	17 08	317	21 08	17	1 08	1 09	1 10	1 11
18	1 12	78	5 12	138	9 12	198	13 12	258	17 12	318	21 12	18	1 12	1 13	1 14	1 15
19	1 16	79	5 16	139	9 16	199	13 16	259	17 16	319	21 16	19	1 16	1 17	1 18	1 19
20	1 20	80	5 20	140	9 20	200	13 20	260	17 20	320	21 20	20	1 20	1 21	1 22	1 23
21	1 24	81	5 24	141	9 24	201	13 24	261	17 24	321	21 24	21	1 24	1 25	1 26	1 27
22	1 28	82	5 28	142	9 28	202	13 28	262	17 28	322	21 28	22	1 28	1 29	1 30	1 31
23	1 32	83	5 32	143	9 32	203	13 32	263	17 32	323	21 32	23	1 32	1 33	1 34	1 35
24	1 36	84	5 36	144	9 36	204	13 36	264	17 36	324	21 36	24	1 36	1 37	1 38	1 39
25	1 40	85	5 40	145	9 40	205	13 40	265	17 40	325	21 40	25	1 40	1 41	1 42	1 43
26	1 44	86	5 44	146	9 44	206	13 44	266	17 44	326	21 44	26	1 44	1 45	1 46	1 47
27	1 48	87	5 48	147	9 48	207	13 48	267	17 48	327	21 48	27	1 48	1 49	1 50	1 51
28	1 52	88	5 52	148	9 52	208	13 52	268	17 52	328	21 52	28	1 52	1 53	1 54	1 55
29	1 56	89	5 56	149	9 56	209	13 56	269	17 56	329	21 56	29	1 56	1 57	1 58	1 59
30	2 00	90	6 00	150	10 00	210	14 00	270	18 00	330	22 00	30	2 00	2 01	2 02	2 03
31	2 04	91	6 04	151	10 04	211	14 04	271	18 04	331	22 04	31	2 04	2 05	2 06	2 07
32	2 08	92	6 08	152	10 08	212	14 08	272	18 08	332	22 08	32	2 08	2 09	2 10	2 11
33	2 12	93	6 12	153	10 12	213	14 12	273	18 12	333	22 12	33	2 12	2 13	2 14	2 15
34	2 16	94	6 16	154	10 16	214	14 16	274	18 16	334	22 16	34	2 16	2 17	2 18	2 19
35	2 20	95	6 20	155	10 20	215	14 20	275	18 20	335	22 20	35	2 20	2 21	2 22	2 23
36	2 24	96	6 24	156	10 24	216	14 24	276	18 24	336	22 24	36	2 24	2 25	2 26	2 27
37	2 28	97	6 28	157	10 28	217	14 28	277	18 28	337	22 28	37	2 28	2 29	2 30	2 31
38	2 32	98	6 32	158	10 32	218	14 32	278	18 32	338	22 32	38	2 32	2 33	2 34	2 35
39	2 36	99	6 36	159	10 36	219	14 36	279	18 36	339	22 36	39	2 36	2 37	2 38	2 39
40	2 40	100	6 40	160	10 40	220	14 40	280	18 40	340	22 40	40	2 40	2 41	2 42	2 43
41	2 44	101	6 44	161	10 44	221	14 44	281	18 44	341	22 44	41	2 44	2 45	2 46	2 47
42	2 48	102	6 48	162	10 48	222	14 48	282	18 48	342	22 48	42	2 48	2 49	2 50	2 51
43	2 52	103	6 52	163	10 52	223	14 52	283	18 52	343	22 52	43	2 52	2 53	2 54	2 55
44	2 56	104	6 56	164	10 56	224	14 56	284	18 56	344	22 56	44	2 56	2 57	2 58	2 59
45	3 00	105	7 00	165	11 00	225	15 00	285	19 00	345	23 00	45	3 00	3 01	3 02	3 03
46	3 04	106	7 04	166	11 04	226	15 04	286	19 04	346	23 04	46	3 04	3 05	3 06	3 07
47	3 08	107	7 08	167	11 08	227	15 08	287	19 08	347	23 08	47	3 08	3 09	3 10	3 11
48	3 12	108	7 12	168	11 12	228	15 12	288	19 12	348	23 12	48	3 12	3 13	3 14	3 15
49	3 16	109	7 16	169	11 16	229	15 16	289	19 16	349	23 16	49	3 16	3 17	3 18	3 19
50	3 20	110	7 20	170	11 20	230	15 20	290	19 20	350	23 20	50	3 20	3 21	3 22	3 23
51	3 24	111	7 24	171	11 24	231	15 24	291	19 24	351	23 24	51	3 24	3 25	3 26	3 27
52	3 28	112	7 28	172	11 28	232	15 28	292	19 28	352	23 28	52	3 28	3 29	3 30	3 31
53	3 32	113	7 32	173	11 32	233	15 32	293	19 32	353	23 32	53	3 32	3 33	3 34	3 35
54	3 36	114	7 36	174	11 36	234	15 36	294	19 36	354	23 36	54	3 36	3 37	3 38	3 39
55	3 40	115	7 40	175	11 40	235	15 40	295	19 40	355	23 40	55	3 40	3 41	3 42	3 43
56	3 44	116	7 44	176	11 44	236	15 44	296	19 44	356	23 44	56	3 44	3 45	3 46	3 47
57	3 48	117	7 48	177	11 48	237	15 48	297	19 48	357	23 48	57	3 48	3 49	3 50	3 51
58	3 52	118	7 52	178	11 52	238	15 52	298	19 52	358	23 52	58	3 52	3 53	3 54	3 55
59	3 56	119	7 56	179	11 56	239	15 56	299	19 56	359	23 56	59	3 56	3 57	3 58	3 59

Conversion of Arc (longitude) to Time

Towing

International Code of Symbols

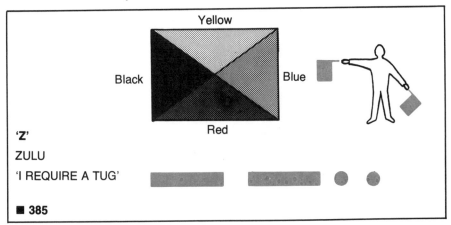

Yellow

Black

Blue

Red

'Z'

ZULU

'I REQUIRE A TUG'

■ 385

Towing signals

By day

A diamond shape where it can best be seen, by both the tug and the tow ■ 386.

By night

When towing, a vessel exhibits *two masthead lights* in a vertical line ■ 387.

If the tow exceeds 200 metres *three masthead lights* are exhibited in a vertical line ■ 388.

■ 387 *Towing signals by night*

■ 386 *Towing signals by day*

■ 388 *Towing signals by night, the tow being more than 200 metres*

232

For towing signals when the length of the tow exceeds 200 metres

If the tug and tow are unable to deviate from their course, then *in addition*, the tug exhibits *red-white-red* lights in a vertical line ■ 389.

■ **389** *Towing signals by night, tug and tow being unable to deviate from course*

At sea

For the tow-boat

Approach the boat in need from her leeward side.

Pass alongside, turn, then throw the tow-line to her as you cross her bow ■ **390**.

To maintain manoeuvrability, fasten the tow-line to a point *forward* of the rudder. Tugboats usually tow from a position near amidships.

A bridle can be tied between the cockpit winches ■ **391**.

A harness can be lashed around the Samson post or mast ■ **392** and the bight run aft.

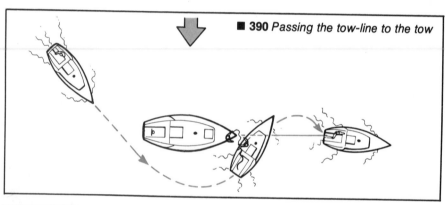

■ **390** *Passing the tow-line to the tow*

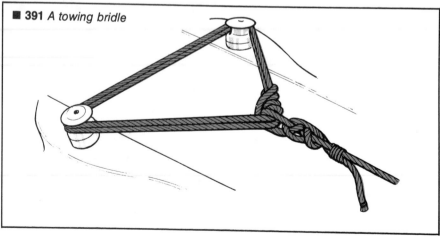

■ **391** *A towing bridle*

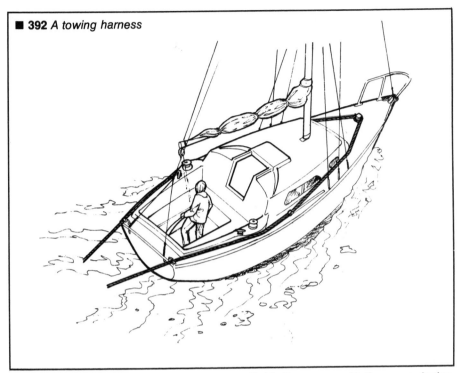

■ **392** *A towing harness*

NOTE:

If two warps need to be joined together, use a carrick bend. **See: Knots**

Always keep a large knife or axe ready in case the tow-line must be cut.

Allow plenty of scope for the tow-rope. It is better to err on the side of having a tow-rope too long, than one too short.

If there is a sea running: The length of the warp should be approximately the wavelength of the sea so that both boats will ride the waves with the same rhythm ■ **393.**

A weight, such as a small anchor or a few metres of chain, shackled to the line will act as a shock absorber.

Begin the tow *only* when the two boats and the tow-rope are on the same axis, that is on a straight line.

Surge any slack in the line around a post or cleat so that the rope does not snap or jerk.

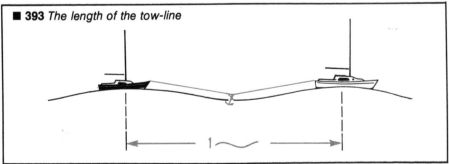

■ **393** *The length of the tow-line*

■ 394 *Using the anchor and anchor chain as a shock absorber*

WARNING:

Always keep tension on the tow-line so that it will not foul the propeller.

The tow-line should be bowsed into a bow fairlead to hold it in place securely, or be guided by a loose lashing to a bow fitting.

If no secure fitting is available, shackle the towline to the anchor or anchor chain and secure it to a strong point. In a heavy swell this can be advantageous as the anchor will act as a shock absorber **■ 394.**

NOTE:

If an agreement concerning a fee for the tow is reached, even verbally, but in the presence of witnesses, this prevents a salvage claim being made later. **See: Salvage**

Legally, the two boats – the tug and the boat being towed – are regarded as one craft. The captain of the tug is in charge.

Establish a clear set of signals with the boat being towed for: *Stop, slow down, go ahead* and *release the line.* **■ 395, 396, 397, 398.**

■ 395 *'CUT! RELEASE THE LINE!'*

396 *'STOP!'*

397 *'GO!'*

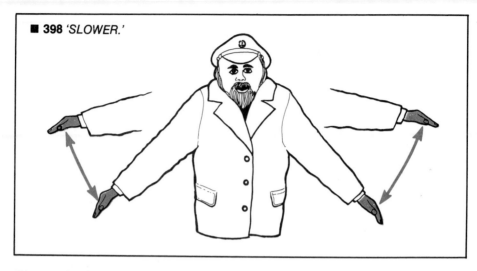

■ **398** *'SLOWER.'*

Communication ■ 399

A long line is attached to a bottle
containing a message. The bottle is
thrown in the tug's wake where it will drift
back and alongside the boat being towed.

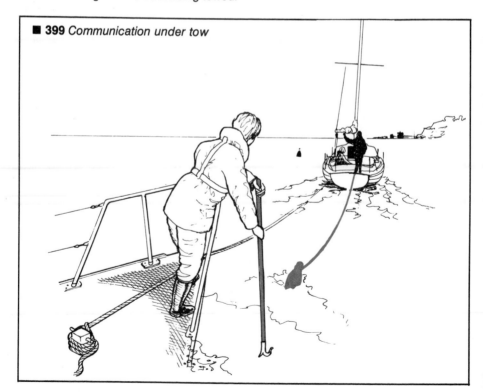

■ **399** *Communication under tow*

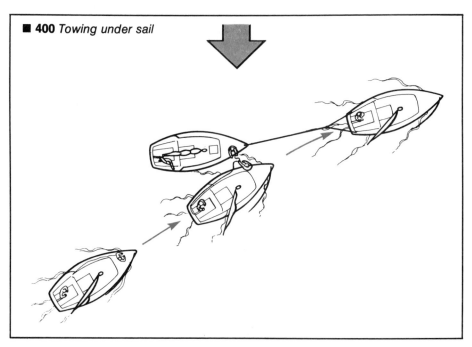

■ **400** *Towing under sail*

Towing under sail ■ 400

Prepare the towline and carry one end forward on the windward side.

Approach the boat to be towed on her leeward side.

Pass over the towline as you cross her bow.

Fall off quickly, as the tension on the line will tend to bring you up into the wind.

NOTE:

Towing under sail can be surprisingly effective. Even larger craft can be towed in this fashion, especially on a reach, broad reach, and down wind.

Towing a school of dinghies ■ 401

Stream a heavy warp with a float at the end.

The dinghies are attached with a slipped stopper knot (rolling hitch).

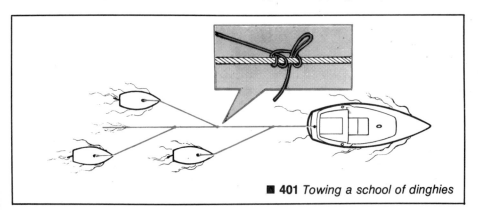

■ **401** *Towing a school of dinghies*

Towing a grounded or stranded craft

If a towline cannot be heaved or taken over by dinghy then from up-wind or up-current, a bight can be floated over attached to a life-jacket, jerry can, fender or mooring buoy.

A long scope should be used.

To prevent falling off, beam-on to the stranded boat, a bow anchor can be set. Winching in the anchor cable, together with the force of the engine and sails, will yield maximum pulling power.

For the boat being towed

The tow-line

This should be made fast to:

The strongest point on the foredeck. On Samson posts and bollards, attach the warp with a tugboat hitch ■ **402.**

The mast at deck level, if it is stepped on the keel.

A bight around the coach roof and/or the cockpit winches ■ **403.**

A lashing joining the mast and both sets of shrouds.

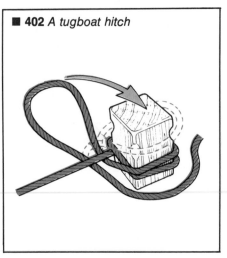

■ **402** *A tugboat hitch*

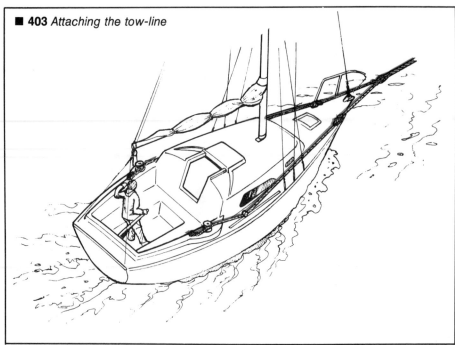

■ **403** *Attaching the tow-line*

A set of oars or spars blocking the forward hatch ■ **404.**

Steer in the wake of the tug

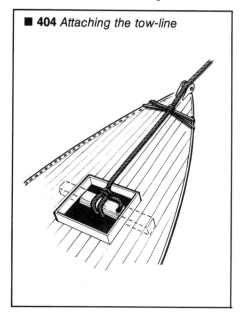

■ **404** *Attaching the tow-line*

To prevent salvage claims
See: Salvage

Agree to a towing fee in advance.

Do not show any emergency or distress flags or signals.

Make the minimum use of warps or aid from the other boat. Merely the acceptance of a tow-line from another boat does *not* automatically entitle that boat to a salvage claim.

Make a detailed entry in the logbook and have the crew sign it.

In harbours and calm waters

Towing alongside ■ 405, 406

Both boats should be adequately protected by fenders. **See: Fenders**

The tow-boat should approach on the lee side of the boat being towed.

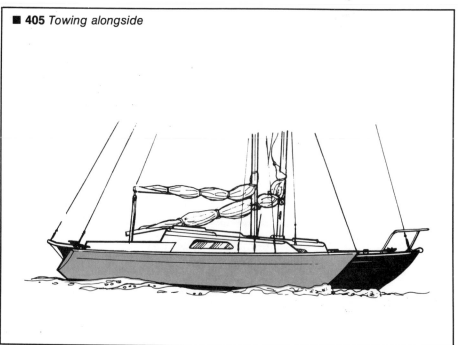

■ **405** *Towing alongside*

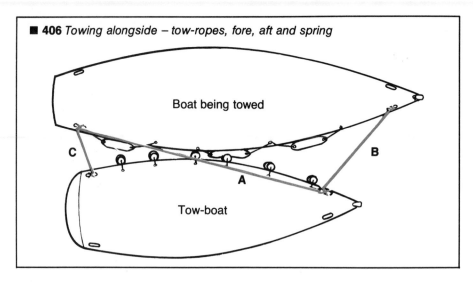

■ **406** *Towing alongside – tow-ropes, fore, aft and spring*

Boat being towed

C

A

B

Tow-boat

Attach lines: ■ **406**

A strong warp from the tow-boat's bow – as a spring – to the stern of the boat being towed ■ **406A.**

From the bow of the tow-boat to the bow of the boat being towed ■ **406B.**

From the stern of the tow-boat to the stern of the boat being towed ■ **406C.**

All lines should be tied as tightly as possible to bind both boats into a single unit.

NOTE:

For maximum steering the rudders of both boats should be used.

WARNING:

Because of the great increase in mass the backing and stopping power of the tow boat's engine will be greatly reduced.

Towing from a dinghy ■ **407**

The warp should be of some floating rope material.

Length: long enough so that it just rises out of the water with each pull from the dinghy.

If too long, force will be lost in friction.

If too short, the rope will jerk with each pull.

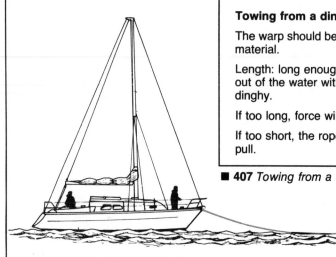

■ **407** *Towing from a dinghy*

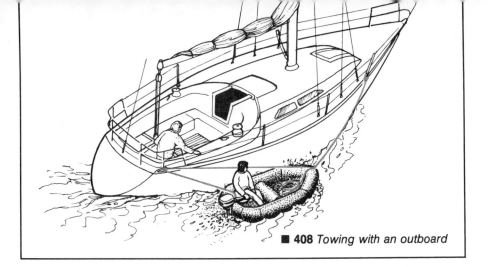

■ **408** *Towing with an outboard*

Towing with an outboard ■ 408

The dinghy must be attached to the quarter of the boat being towed.

Attach lines:

From the bow of the dinghy to the stern of the boat being towed.

From the stern of the dinghy to the stern of the boat being towed.

From the bow of the dinghy to the forward quarter of the boat being towed.

The dinghy will only provide thrust. The boat must be steered.

Towing from shore ■ 409

The tow-rope should *not* be fastened to the stem, even if someone is at the helm. The boat will still have a strong tendency to sheer shorewards.

Instead, the tow-rope should be fastened somewhere near the mast, a chain plate, for example, which is usually just forward of the centre of pivot.

If there are obstacles between the path and the boat, the tow-rope should be looped around the mast, then hoisted to the hounds to clear the obstacle.

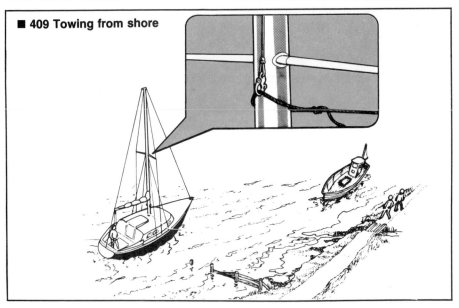

■ **409 Towing from shore**

Tranquillizers

Tranquillizers can separate the perception of pain from the reaction to pain. By calming the sensation of pain, the reaction becomes less severe.

NOTE:

When taking tranquillizers, do *not* drink alcohol.

	Dosage
England	
Valium	5–10mg./ 6hrs.

	Dosage
France	
Valium	5–10mg./ 6hrs.

	Dosage
Germany	
Valium	5–10mg./ 6hrs.

Turnbuckles

See: Bottle screws

Typhoons

See: Law of storms

Tropical jelly fish stings

Treatment

Using gloves or rags for protection, remove any tentacles at once.

Treat for shock if necessary. **See: Shock**

Wash the area with fresh water and well-diluted ammonia.

Coat the area with a bicarbonate of soda paste.

Administer an antihistamine.

	Dosage
England	
Piriton	4mg. 3–4 times per day

	Dosage
France	
Polaramine	2mg. 3–4 times per day

	Dosage
Germany	
Tavegil	1mg. 3–4 times a day

U

Urine

In survival conditions

Urine should *not* be drunk. It will not replace lost body fluids.

More than likely, urine will become concentrated, turn dark and be painful to pass. However, this is not harmful.

In emergencies urine can be used as an antiseptic.

Vitamins

The four major vitamins

1 – Vitamin 'A'

A deficiency results in
Night blindness.
Dry, flaky skin.
Brittle, falling hair.
A susceptibility to infectious diseases.

Common sources of Vitamin 'A' are
Green vegetables (particularly watercress and parsley), carrots and apricots.
Cod liver oil.
Whole milk.

2 – 'B' Complex

A deficiency results in
Nervousness.
Fatigue.
Headaches.
Insomnia.
Wind and constipation.

Common sources of 'B' Complex Vitamins are
Whole grain foods.
Milk and yogurt.

Liver.
Leafy green vegetables.
Brewer's yeast.

3 – Vitamin 'C'

A deficiency results in
General fatigue.
Mild depression.
Headaches and aching limbs.
Eventually scurvy. **See: Scurvy**

Common sources of Vitamin 'C' are
Nearly every fresh vegetable and fruit.
Especially citrus fruits.

4 – Vitamin 'D'

A deficiency results in
Poor absorption of calcium and phosphorus, which are essential for strong bones and teeth.

Common sources of Vitamin 'D' are
Milk and butter.
Eggs.
Fish oils.
Fresh green vegetables.

Water

At sea, fresh water can be obtained from

Rainwater collection. **See: Rainwater**

A solar still. **See: Solar still**

Distillation. **See: Distillation**

Taking on water

Use your own hose, if possible.

NOTE:

To prevent the growth of bacteria, after each use the hose should be drained, dried and plugged.

If using someone else's hose, flush it out for at least a full minute.

Purification

Household bleach

For clear water, two drops per litre.

For cloudy water, four drops per litre.

2% tincture of iodine

For clear water, five drops per litre.

For cloudy water, 10 drops per litre.

Let the water stand for at least a half-hour before using.

Pouring the water back and forth between containers will aerate and remove much of the chlorine smell.

Weather forecast

Barometer

Stable: stable weather.

Rising slowly: good weather ahead.

Falling slowly: wind, and a further, faster fall.

Falling quickly: (more than one millibar per hour) – stormy weather.

Admiral Fitzroy's rules

The barometer rises for a northerly wind (including NW and NE), for dry or less wet weather, for less wind, or for more than one of these changes – except when rain or snow comes from the north with a strong wind.

The barometer falls for a south wind (including SE and SW), for wet weather, for stronger wind, or for more than one of these changes, except when a moderate wind with rain or snow comes from the north.

'Long foretold, long last;
Short warning, soon past.'

Temperature

A normal curve

Rising in the morning, then falling again after noon: good weather.

In summer

Quickly rising temperature: good weather.
Quickly falling temperature: bad weather.

In winter

Quickly rising temperature: bad weather.
Quickly falling temperature: good weather.

Wind

A sudden change in direction after several days of constant wind means bad weather.

An increasing wind in the morning, and a decreasing wind in the afternoon means good weather.

An increasing wind in the afternoon or evening means storm and rain.

The wind following the sun, that is, from the east in the morning and from the west in the evening means good weather.

The wind 'backing' against the sun, until it is east in the evening means bad weather.

Clouds

Clouds in layers and at different levels means changeable weather.

Cumulus in the morning and less in the afternoon and evening means bad weather.

Gathering altostratus clouds means an approaching warm front with rain.

Spotted altocumulus means continued good weather.

'Mares' tails' with little motion means gales from the direction they radiate from.

Sunrise

Red: bad weather.

Clear, but with a reddish touch: bad weather.

Sunset

Red: good weather.

Clear behind cumulus clouds: good weather.

Bright yellow: wind.

Pale yellow or green: rain.

Moon

Silver and light: good weather.

A ring or halo: wind and rain.

Sea life

Sea-birds far out to sea: good weather.

Sea-birds flying inland: bad weather.

Vast quantities of jelly fish: good weather.

Porpoises in shallow water: bad weather.

Phosphorescent sea: good weather.

See: Law of storms

Wind

See: Law of storms, weather forecast

Wood repair

For cracks or holes in plywood hulls ■ 410, 411

Cut the damaged area into a square hole.

Cut a marine plywood plug – preferably the same thickness as the hull – to fit the hole exactly.

Cut a backing plate at least 5cm. larger than the hole on all sides.

Glue (epoxy) and screw/nail the backing plate to the inside of the hull. For larger holes battens should be used instead of a backing plate.

Glue and screw/nail the plug into place.

For additional strength a layer of glass fibre can be moulded over the backing plate. **See: Glass fibre repair**

NOTE:

Since the two outside layers of marine plywood are the hardest (those with the dark grain), they should not be sanded too much.

■ **412**

■ **413**

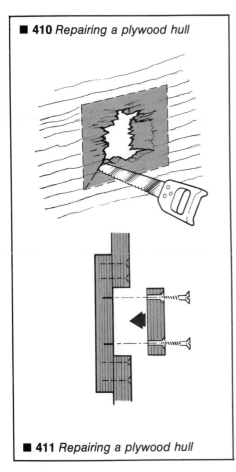

■ **410** *Repairing a plywood hull*

■ **411** *Repairing a plywood hull*

For cracks or holes in planked hulls

Patches ■ 412

Cut a wooden patch which will overlap the damaged area by at least 10cm.

Cover the inside of the patch with mastic, bedding compound, or sealer. If none is available, a rag, towel, or sailcloth well greased or soaked in paint, primer or bitumen will serve as well.

Screw or nail the patch in place, carefully sealing the leading edges.

NOTE:

For irregular surfaces, such as those found on a clinker hull, a tingle may have to be used. This can be cut from sheet lead or copper and easily beaten into shape. The tingle is screwed or nailed in place in the same manner as a patch ■ **413.**

For cracks, weak, damaged or leaky areas

Glass fibre

Materials
See: Glass fibre repair

Procedure

NOTE:

Glass fibre will form a secure bond with wood, but only if the wooden surface is carefully prepared.

Remove any old paint or varnish. Paint remover or sanding is the best method. Burning off old paint is likely to drive oils into the wood which may prevent a strong bond. The final surface should be smooth, but not overly so. All sharp edges should be rounded in order to prevent air bubbles from forming under the mat.

Paint the bare wood with enough coats of activated resin to fill in the grain. Let the area dry, then sand it lightly.

Cut the cloth or mat to fit the area. Several layers will be necessary, and their weave patterns should be criss-crossed.

Wet the first layer thoroughly with resin. Before it begins to cure, add the next layer. Use a roller or bottle to squeeze out any air bubbles which would become weak points.

Add one or two additional coats of resin to fill in the pores of the last layer and provide a smooth finish.

Wounds

Three immediate dangers
Bleeding. **See: Haemorrhages**

Shock. **See: Shock**

Infection which could lead to blood poisoning.

Treatment

Stop the bleeding by applying a sterile dressing. This should not be too tight. If firm at first to stop the bleeding, it should be loosened later.

If possible, elevate the injured part.

Do not

Touch it.

Leave it exposed to the air.

Remove any glass or metal fragments unless they are superficial and can be easily lifted out.

If the wound is large and open

Hold it closed with a plaster or pack it with sterile gauze. After the bleeding has stopped, with clean hands, sew it closed with a sterilized sail needle (the smallest one available). **See: Sterilization**

If the wound is deep and gaping, stitch the flesh together with cat gut then close the skin with silk. Holding the needle with forceps or pliers, make one stitch at a time, tying off each one with a granny knot. Clip off the ends.

NOTE:

Sewing a wound closed is usually not unbearably painful. It is normal that quite a bit of blood will flow while the sewing is taking place.

If the wound is closed, such as a bruise

Salt water compresses will have a soothing effect and reduce swelling. But they should *not* be used for open wounds.

Postscript

Yachtsman's Emergency Handbook is
by no means complete. It cannot be. In
any crisis situation, particularly one at
sea, the variables are so many, so
unpredictable, and often so subjective
that a full accounting is an impossibility. A
great many people have contributed their
sea wisdom, and an enormous amount of
time has gone into the collation of data
but we see this book only as a starting
point from which we will continue to
collect the test solutions in the hope that
the next time this book goes to press the
body of emergency knowledge will be
more complete.

In this task we welcome any suggestions,
criticisms, corrections or additions any
sailor has to offer.

The Authors
Koblenz
1979

Index